LEADERSHIP

in the

CRUCIBLE

of

WORK

 FLORIDA
HOSPITAL
Since 1908

LEADERSHIP

in the

CRUCIBLE

of

WORK

DISCOVERING *the* INTERIOR LIFE
of an AUTHENTIC LEADER

SANDY SHUGART, PhD

FLORIDA
HOSPITAL

LEADERSHIP IN THE CRUCIBLE OF WORK
Copyright © 2013 Sandy Shugart
Published by Florida Hospital Publishing
605 Montgomery Road,
Altamonte Springs, Florida 32714

To EXTEND *the* HEALTH *and* HEALING MINISTRY *of* CHRIST

EDITOR-IN-CHIEF:	Todd Chobotar
MANAGING EDITOR:	David Biebel, DMin
INTERNAL PEER REVIEW:	Brian Paradis, CPA, CMA
	Bill Largo, MDiv
EXTERNAL PEER REVIEW:	Margie McCombs, PhD
	Barbara Olsen, MACL
PRODUCTION:	Lillian Boyd
PROMOTION:	Caryn McCleskey
COPY EDITOR:	Pamela Nordberg
ART DIRECTOR:	Rob Birkhead
PHOTOGRAPHER:	Spencer Freeman
DESIGN:	Golden Spiral Creative

For volume discounts please contact special sales at:
HealthProducts@FLHosp.org | 407-200-8224

Library of Congress Control Number: 2012950446
Printed in the United States of America.
PR 14 13 12 11 10 9 8 7 6 5 4 3
ISBN: 978-0-9839881-9-9

For more life-changing resources visit:
FloridaHospitalPublishing.com
CreationHealth.com

CONTENTS

"The unexamined life

is not worth living."

~ Socrates

PRELUDE

IN THE CRUCIBLE

A T A VERY YOUNG AGE, I WAS THROWN INTO THE deep end of the pool. Whether by providence or fluke, at age twenty-five, I became a senior leader in a very large organization—a multi-layered, hierarchical, political, billion-dollar enterprise. Without ever seeking it out, with no real ambition for this kind of leadership, I found myself immersed in the competitive, power-laden, palace politics of a modern bureaucracy— for which I was totally unprepared. My interests were music, poetry, theology, philosophy, natural history, learning, and most deeply of all, I wanted to be of service to others. I was trying to discern a vocation in teaching, ordained ministry, higher education, missions. Yet, I found myself in staff meetings, before legislative committees, defending decisions to other senior officers and constituents, wrestling with human resource issues. In short, I was becoming a bureaucrat. I wondered if I would survive. I wasn't paralyzed by the thought; it all seemed like a temporary job to me anyway. But I did wonder.

Meanwhile, I kept my ears open, asked a lot of questions, and kept my mouth shut (well, for me it was rather shut, though to others I must have seemed very free with my opinions). Instead of failing, I learned and grew, mastering much of the content of the job and finding I had a knack for the politics. I learned the game and got rather good at it. Before long, I became known as the "golden boy" of the organization—a promising up-and-comer. The mastery, the reputation, the praise were all very gratifying, and my confidence grew. Still, my deep desire was to serve, and I told myself that mastering the game of bureaucratic leadership, the palace politics, would position me to be of greater service.

I was becoming someone I didn't want to be. And it was happening at work.

Then one day, in the midst of my success, something important happened. I hurt someone. I injured a colleague at work, one I really cared for. I did it in a time-honored tradition: in a staff meeting. I can't recall after all these years exactly what I did. Perhaps I withheld some information from her, sprang it on her in the meeting rather than sharing it in advance. Maybe

I attempted to prove how bright I was by dismantling her logic in public. Likely, I just went for a laugh and touched her in a place that was infinitely more sensitive than I knew.

At any rate, I hurt her. And rather than swallowing the humiliation like most of us do at work, only to see it resurface in some unrelated part of our lives, she gave me a great and precious gift. She followed me back to my office, closed the door, and gave full vent to her rage. Her point was simple and undeniable. My behavior wasn't consistent with my values. "You're not who you say you are. You're not who you *think* you are!" And all I could do was agree and apologize.

It was a rude awakening. I spent some sleepless nights wrestling with what it meant. My friend had held up a mirror to me and I didn't like what I saw, although I did recognize it as me. I wasn't who I thought I was. More to the point, I was *becoming* someone I didn't want to be. And it was happening at work. In a rare flash of insight, I realized that the jerks—the old burned-out, negative, manipulating, officious, self-centered bureaucrats about whom we all made jokes—*started out just like me.* They hadn't always been jerks. Well, some of them hadn't always been jerks. And I was headed toward a certain future of distorted humanity, a deep malformation of

For most leaders in an imperfect, broken world, the crucible is unavoidable.

character, if I didn't figure out how this was happening to me.

I thought about my alternatives. Perhaps I should change jobs, careers even; find a place where there wasn't so much of the politics, power, and pressure. Couldn't I escape such a corrosive work environment? Except that the place I worked, in comparison to many others, wasn't so bad. It was, in fact, better than most. As I looked around for alternatives, I found precious few places that didn't share the same problem to some degree. The more I contemplated the problem, the less escapable it seemed to be. Still further, I didn't get the feeling that I was supposed to escape. Rather, what grew in me was a sense that I was meant to be in places just like this. There was something for me to learn, something for me to contribute here. But how could I do this without being ruined?

In the months of reflection that followed, a metaphor arose for me that I have found helpful: the crucible. Trained as a chemist, I knew that a crucible was a hardened ceramic vessel in which to perform reactions that would shatter an ordinary Pyrex flask with too much heat, pressure, reactivity, corrosive by-products. Heat, pressure, reactivity, corrosive by-products: to me, this sounded like work, my work. Not every minute of every day, but often. The threat of the crucible of work is always in the background, especially for *leaders*: those who have accepted heightened responsibility for others and for the performance of their organization; those who live with accountability for many variables that are out of their control; those who are tempted, in fact taught, to assert control using the tools of power and hierarchy at their disposal; those who face the possibility of very public failure; and those who receive the often exaggerated rewards of success and are tempted to believe these rewards are *owed* to them.

Both people in leadership in elite organizations and people in ordinary, everyday jobs experience the heat, pressure, reactivity, and corrosion of the crucible. The redoubtable Studs Terkel recorded this much in his powerful account of interviews with ordinary working Americans:

> This book, being about work, is, by its very nature, about violence—to the spirit as well as to the body. It is about ulcers as well as accidents, about shouting matches as well as fistfights, about nervous breakdowns as well as kicking the dog around. It is, above all (or beneath all), about daily humiliations. To survive the day is triumph enough for the walking wounded among the great many of us (*Work*, Studs Terkel).

If this is true for many at work, what price do they pay deep in their hearts and characters? Who are they becoming every day at work? And how much more true might this be of those who lead, who live in the magnified heat, pressure, reactivity, and corrosion of elevated responsibility? Even if they aren't experiencing the crucible themselves, what responsibility might they bear for helping to create the crucible in which others are compelled to work?

This was my great epiphany and the foundation for this book: for most leaders in an imperfect, broken world, the crucible is unavoidable. There is no opting out. There are times, of course, when the work is going so well that the crucible isn't actually looming before you, but just when you think you've got everything calmed down, working smoothly, under control, all hell breaks loose and you're back in the crucible. My question was this: How might I endure the crucible without being hopelessly deformed by it? And as a leader, how might I shape the crucible for others to something less harmful?

Instead of being deformed in the heat of the crucible, might a leader be purified and formed, like bronze, into something more valuable?

Then the metaphor shifted. (That's what good metaphors do,

revealing something we didn't realize we knew through the connections they help us make.) I recalled that there was another, older meaning to *crucible*. It comes from one of the first real technologies of civilization— metallurgy. Civilized societies took root when someone discovered how to make bronze, a metal that could be worked and given an edge for, say, a plowshare, sickle, or hoe. Native copper could be removed from its rock matrix by heating it to 1,083 degrees Celsius. Its impurities removed, the liquid metal was ready to be cast. And if there was a little of the element tin in the rock, it alloyed the copper into what we call bronze, a harder and more useful metal that could be worked and given an edge for cutting harder materials, like wood or an opponent's shield.

If the heat and pressure and reactivity of the crucible of leadership can't be removed, if they are a part of human society and collective work—an important reason why leadership is required—might there be a way to engage the crucible that is more productive?

Instead of being deformed in the heat of the crucible, might a leader be purified and *formed*, like bronze, into something more valuable, more useful?

How, then, could I approach my own work and create a work environment for others that was *formative*?

A leader's first work, her most important and enduring work, is her interior work.

In the essays that follow, you are invited to reflect on these questions as they present themselves at the places and in the substance of your work. The premise is that the crucible is unavoidable and that the only way to direct the heat and pressure of the crucible toward something positive, toward formation, is by doing interior work. It is here, in the leader's character and spirit, that the effects of the crucible, for good or ill, are first experienced and ultimately transmitted through leadership responsibilities to the lives of others. So a leader's first work, her most important and enduring work, is her interior work, to attend to what is happening in her own character, attitudes, and habits of thought, to know her assumptions, even as they are being formed and reformed. Then her job is to connect her interior work to her exterior work, so what she does in the world is an expression of her true and emerging self. This connectedness—exterior work flowing from and contributing to interior formation—is what we really mean by integrity. It is what makes some leaders, for lack of a better term, authentic.

Some years later in my pilgrimage as a leader, I discovered yet another meaning in the metaphor of the crucible. This one comes not from chemistry or metallurgy, but from alchemy. Flourishing in the late Middle Ages, alchemy was an amalgam of magic, philosophy, and early science. One of its central and most symbolic principles was the belief in the rarest of all substances, the philosopher's stone, which represented wisdom in material form. Alchemists believed that if a small bit of the philosopher's stone were heated with a quantity of an *ignoble* or base metal, like lead, the base metal would be transmuted, transformed into a *noble* metal, like gold. This process of turning lead into gold, ignoble to noble, was carried out in a crucible.

Here is an even more powerful metaphor:

- What if work, especially the work of leadership, could be *transforming*?

- What if the crucible could be engaged with such wisdom that we would be not only formed for service but transformed for goodness?
- Romantic though this may sound, still it is powerfully attractive. How wonderful would it be if we were, all of us, enlarged by our work, not diminished? Who wouldn't want to be, at the end of the day, nourished by our work, not depleted?
- Wouldn't we all want, over the trajectory of our careers, to have been on a significant journey, not just caught up in a rat race?

The secret ingredient, the philosopher's stone, the wisdom that leads to transformation is a matter of transcendent purpose.

Here the interior work of formation takes another step, beyond connection to our exterior work to connection to some great work, the difference we want to make in the universe. Perhaps this sounds a bit grandiose, but aren't we most drawn to another whose journey has meaning because it reaches beyond the here and now? The leaders I admire most were persons whose lives left for others a legacy of courage, meaning, love, and purpose. Some of the reflections that follow will test even this thin air.

A Word on Organization

This is not a how-to book. It has been written after years of public speaking and private mentoring on these subjects in response to an expressed desire from audiences to have a way to continue the conversation. I can't offer you a template for your growth and success at work. I can't even instruct you on how to do your interior work. Each of us discovers her own personal workshop in her own way. What I can offer you is this invitation to enter the conversation concerning how we form and are formed by our work.

This conversation requires some particularity since the issues we confront at work are always concrete. So the essays are based on a variety of issues and questions taken separately but connected by the image of the crucible and the agency of the philosopher's stone, the wisdom of ongoing self-inquiry.

The conversation also requires something of a paradoxical character, a balance of opposites. As my old favorite uncle used to advise, "There's a ditch on both sides of the road, Son." So, as you can see from the table of contents, I have organized these reflections into paired essays considering two sides of our formative experiences of work. I chose these particular themes because they have seemed both important and neglected categories for us to consider.

What if work, especially the work of leadership, could be transforming?

If the essays that follow stir up your conversation with yourself and with others, if they trouble you a bit, if they manage to raise questions you cannot easily dismiss, I will consider my purpose fulfilled.

Sometimes

Sometimes
if you move carefully
through the forest
breathing
like the ones
in the old stories
who could cross
a shimmering bed of dry leaves
without a sound,
you come
to a place
whose only task
is to trouble you
with tiny
but frightening requests
conceived out of nowhere
but in this place
beginning to lead everywhere
requests to stop what
you are doing right now,
and
to stop what you
are becoming
while you do it,
questions
that can make
or unmake
a life,
questions
that have patiently
waited for you,
questions that have no right
to go away.

David Whyte
Everything is Waiting for You

FORMED BY WORK

FORMING THE WORK

FORMED BY WORK

THE CONSEQUENCES OF CONTROL

OUR WORK FORMS US MORE POWERFULLY THAN we form it. The daily, hourly assumptions, objectives, habits, skills, and tools that make it possible for us to produce good, competent work aren't just working on raw material, whether brick and mortar or an empty page or a corporate balance sheet. What we do and what we use to do it, shapes us, as well. There's a reason why a carpenter's handshake comes to be shaped like the handle of a hammer. It isn't surprising that a finance officer sees much of the world in terms of a spreadsheet. It is difficult not to notice how many architects keep their notes on sketch pads and graph paper.

Once, a long time ago, we knew something of this connection. People were even given names that reflected their craft—that is, the tools they used to make a living—and in some ways their character and place in the world. Fisher, Gardener, Smith, Shepherd, Wagoner, Tinker: names had a deeper significance then. Even our ancient traditions of faith remind us that deep identity and name have long been connected. Abraham means *father of a multitude*; Isaac means *one who laughs*; Jacob means *deceiver*. And these names, these deep identities, were inscribed on them by no one less than the creator and Lord of their universe.

In some ways, names based on guild, craft, or even on cosmic destiny represented, I suppose, limitations, the boundaries of class and privilege or proper place in the scheme of things. But they also indicated purpose, gifts, and how a person was likely to view and behave in the world, a deeper connection between what she was about and who she was becoming. Such names are

> *Our work forms us more powerfully than we form it.*

anachronistic now, vestigial in both purpose and use. But the underlying truth is worth remembering: *what we do shapes our deep identity and character.*

In the modern era, as work has become more complex, titles have become more generic. A worker may not be a cobbler but an executive in retail distribution through which shoes, among other things, are marketed and sold. The title "executive" tells us little about the person who holds it. Even less so does manager, supervisor, or, heaven help us, director of client services. Some titles still contain deeper personal content, such as in the helping professions: nurse, teacher, doctor, sheriff. They at least evoke a sense of common commitment to a profession and its mission. But even in these, the technical differences among specialties and the amazing diversity of environments in which these roles are applied lead us to conclude there is as much diversity within each profession as there is among them.

For leaders in any profession or organization, however, there are expectations of technique, disposition, and performance that amount to a body of professional norms and practices, a professional culture over and above the technical content and competence of their particular fields. Else, why engage in studies of leadership at all? It may be useful to reflect on the kinds of techniques and tools that leaders, those who take on particular responsibility for others and for an enterprise, have in common and to wonder, at least, how their constant use might be shaping the deeper identity of the leader.

What we do shapes our deep identity and character.

THE TOOLS OF LEADERSHIP

The first assumption of leadership is the sense of somehow being in charge of something. We think we are in control. We think we are agents of change. We try to apply a lifetime of knowledge, skill, and competence to complex work problems to produce solutions, meet goals, give a return on investment, preserve and advance the enterprise. Isn't this what they hired us for? Isn't this why they asked us to lead?

Certainly, technique and competence count. All other things being equal, we'd rather our leaders have profound skills, be experts in their fields, know how things work and how to make them work better. Beyond this, though, we want in our leaders a broader set of competencies: the ability to know the truth of our present situation and to see clearly into the future; to plan toward both a large shared vision and specific goals; to execute a plan by coordinating the work of others, delegating effectively and managing the performance of the team for the larger enterprise; to allocate resources intelligently, know the business model and use it to get results; to communicate effectively and advocate persuasively; and to use the tools of business and leadership skillfully to do all these things. Surely, competence counts.

Of course, being competent doesn't always put a person in charge. Many who appear to be in charge are manifestly incompetent. And there are others who lead with great competence but in an environment where most of the important variables are beyond anyone's control, where neither success nor failure may be attributable to competence or the lack of it. In what sense is a great brain surgeon really in charge of an advanced tumor? Or the patient's health? She can only do what she is trained to do, to engage in best professional practice, and hope for the best outcome; to apply with great skill the tools she has mastered—scalpel, medications, proton beams, whatever—and expect the results to be dependent also on many variables she doesn't control.

As a leader, though, this same physician has other kinds of competencies we expect her to employ. For example, to know how to assist the patient with navigating an immensely complex healthcare system to get the best care possible. Or to make the Goliath of a modern hospital attend to the particular needs of an individual patient. Could there be a more complex organizational challenge? And for this work, the years of technical training as a surgeon are only of modest help. Now the competencies that must be employed include such things as understanding how a complex bureaucracy behaves; knowing the regulatory environment of the healthcare industry and applying the rules to the benefit of a patient and his outcomes; persuading others to do more than the standard procedures anticipated and working in complex multidisciplinary teams; knowing how to break the rules when necessary; and occasionally doing battle with those who represent a competing interest that might put the patient at risk.

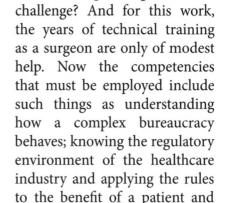

A skilled leader who has mastered the techniques of the craft works like a seasoned craftsman.

This sort of scenario can be described for most leaders. There is technical content they have labored hard to learn and apply, but there is also a more general content associated with working in complex organizations and with a great variety of persons that must be mastered. The tools employed here are harder to define but no less important to the effective performance of the job. They include, among others, power, persuasion, stealth, rank, informal influence, politics, nuanced communication, negotiation, timing, bluffing, and calling bluffs. These, no less than planning and execution, are the tools of most modern organizational leaders, of those who are "in charge."

SHAPED BY THE TOOLS OF LEADERSHIP

If the tools we use to shape our work every day are also shaping us, what effect does the exercise of these other competencies, those associated with being in charge, have on the leader who feels compelled, of necessity, to use them?

The first thing to notice is that most of these more general tools of leadership are aimed at other people. The use of power to gain compliance is a supremely human interaction. A leader doesn't exercise power over things; she just manipulates them. It's all right to manipulate things, systems, and mechanisms to get desired outcomes, assuming doing so isn't breaking the law or breaching ordinary ethics. But the power that leaders wield, if they choose to wield it, is over people.

Similarly, persuasion, influence, communication, and politics are about moving people in some desired direction. The leader may be looking for compliance with some plan, commitment to some goal, capitulation from an opponent, investment from an ally, or any number of other human outcomes. Whatever the leader is trying to achieve, the effort of leadership is aimed at people.

Many seasoned leaders do this work so well it seems effortless, like a great athlete performing in her sport. Indeed, much like a fine athlete, the exercise of these faculties of leadership becomes almost second nature, engaged without really thinking about it much. Or perhaps more to the point, a skilled leader who has mastered the techniques of the craft works like a seasoned craftsman, moving quickly and efficiently in habituated, almost mindless motion, like a brick mason swiftly laying brick to a line without even thinking about it, or the aching back and rough hands the work is giving him. And this mindlessness is where the great risk lies.

When we use people like objects, negative consequences result for them and also for those doing the manipulation.

People are not raw material, not parts in a mechanism, not a system. We may objectify them with impersonal collective nouns like "workforce" or "markets," but they are not, ultimately, objects to be moved and manipulated in the pursuit of some larger objective. They are *persons* who have value, wills, and destinies of their own. When we use them like objects, negative consequences result for them and also for those doing the manipulation. Over time, the loss of a deep sense of the sacredness of other persons cuts the perpetrator off from genuine relationships with anyone. The alienation is slow but sure, and devastating over the life of a leader.

Not only are the leader's relationships at work false, strained, un-nourishing, and bent, but the habits of manipulation and power refuse to be confined to just one area of the "people-user's" life. Relationships in other spheres of life, all other spheres of life, begin to take on the same character of struggle and falsehood. Precisely because control, coercion, and manipulation get such immediate results, they create a powerful cycle of operant conditioning on the leader. Their use is diabolically reinforced and therefore becomes more frequent, more habitual. In the end, the isolation of the leader addicted to these techniques, using them habitually and mindlessly, can be terrible.

The consequences for the leader and for her enterprise are almost always dissatisfying and often deeply disturbing. Most tragic is the leader who knows better, who can see the negative consequences of his own behavior, but can't break the power of the habit, the cycle that has served his short-term purposes so effectively, even when long-term failure is all but guaranteed. Examples in our own work lives abound.

I know a leader of a great servant institution in our own community whose organization has been so damaged by the toxicity of his habits of control and manipulation that no one can work there long without sustaining permanent wounds. Outwardly, he projects competence, wisdom, even servanthood, but his staff knows him as a deeply conflicted and punishing leader. His own unhappiness in this miserable condition only adds to the vitriol waiting to be unleashed when anyone fails to comply with his ever-shifting expectations. His organization seems from the outside to be effective enough, until we consider what might have been, what creative possibilities have been crushed, and what gifted colleagues have been exiled. And he is gradually awakening to the prison he himself has fashioned. How sad.

In the Crucible of Leadership

So here is our crucible experience. In our daily work we are enjoined to use a set of tools that are essential to the enterprise and exercise of leadership, but they are inherently dangerous to both the leader and the led.

How, then, can we prevent the harm this may cause? And how might we engage this same work in ways that have positive, even transformative, consequences for ourselves and others? Where is the philosopher's stone, the wisdom, for this crucible?

If you are looking for a procedure, a formula, I can't help you. Wisdom can't be reduced to a formula. As one traveler to another, I can share some of what I've learned from the road, but you have to navigate for yourself.

Wisdom begins with awareness. Just knowing, becoming conscious of the nature of the tools we are using and how they can affect us is a very good beginning and worthy of continual reflection and self-examination. Some do this work of reflection in a journal; others give themselves a good talking to on a long walk or a run; still others have found or created relationships for accountability, friends who can ask the hard questions and receive our answers both skeptically and unconditionally. The point is to do the interior work and to make all the day-to-day details and signposts of our work the raw material for these self-inquiries.

As unpleasant as it may be, from time to time, gaze boldly into the mirror others hold up to you.

In this process, we do well to look for signs of erosion and growth in our characters through the ways we are engaging our work. Signs of erosion, for example, might be when our approaches to accountability begin to slide slowly toward coercion, or when persuasion becomes spin, or proper discretion moves toward stealth or even ambush, or when negotiation begins to look like manipulation. Pay attention to your feelings in this process: what makes you angry, what delights you, what do idle daydreams reveal about the condition of your heart? Feelings can lead to very productive inquiry. Also, as unpleasant as it may be, from time to time, gaze boldly into the mirror others hold up to you.

You may well find that you feel a little hamstrung by this at first. After all, rivals and competitors are using these tools without compunction and are often gaining a competitive advantage. Perhaps. But I'm asking you to have a little faith that wisdom will lead where shrewdness cannot: to work and places of work that can become, in spite of all our human frailties, places to grow into maturity and grace, much to the long-term benefit of ourselves, our co-workers, and even the enterprise itself.

Brick Work

It wasn't a work I had chosen, but
I was young and the job came to hand
like each new, rasp-edged brick
and I was taken with the
challenge of the craft.
Head-down to lay to a line
straight and square, feeling the
grain of baked earth and
handling the sanded mud with
quick, smart flicks and jabs,
a precision boxer working a square ring,
mastering tools and letting them
master me: hammer, level and trowel.
Focusing, focusing until every
cell is in the rhythm, speed,
economy of motion, each brick
leading to the next, no hesitation,
no space between the notes and
all notes the same,
brick to brick, course on course,
year stacked on
year until I take on the very
texture of brick, the grit of mortar
rigid joints and flat face of the wall
no view but the brick,
no plan but the brick,
no dream but the brick
and then
the walls, at last,
connect and there is
nothing to do but to set the
iron bars in the
tiny, high window
and wait for
the end.

Sandy Shugart

FORMING THE WORK

☙☙☙

THE ILLUSION OF CONTROL

I HAVE A FRIEND WHO IS CONDUCTOR OF A MAJOR symphony orchestra. He likes to say that his role is the "last bastion of unfettered dictatorship in the modern world." Our work may form us, as the previous essay claims, but here is a supreme example of a leader who forms his work. Consider the power of the conductor. Seen from one point of view, he is, in fact, a complete autocrat. He raises the baton and all eyes are fixed on him. Only he has the entire score for the symphony before him; everyone else has only parts. And the parts must come together precisely to make the whole. He controls the rhythm, the tempo. At his urging, the music crescendos or decrescendos. With a glance, he brings in a whole new section of the orchestra.

If the score is to be interpreted intelligently, all must accede to his vision and execute according to his direction. Assuring such compliance is the job of the section leaders, the sort of middle management of the orchestra. We can't have the *concertmeister* leading the violins off in another direction. She must bring them into alignment with the music the conductor already hears in her head. Both in rehearsal and in performance, the will of the conductor is absolute.

This is a unique role. It is very different from, say, the first violin in a quartet whose role is more *primus inter pares*, first among equals. The interpretation of chamber music, the vision for the performance, is something worked out among the players. Their chemistry is vital to the performance: They have to fit together organically to perform musically. I suppose this is true of any ensemble, whether a cello-piano duet playing a sonata, or a rock band improvising on a groove, or a small company of actors developing a play for performance. The work is synergistic and co-created, and these groups typically comprise a small number, say two to ten players.

Persistent Myth: If we can just get the right leader, all will be well.

A symphony orchestra, however, may have more than one hundred players, including at times some very unusual instruments—a celesta, for example—and some that are normally thought of as solo instruments, such as a pipe organ or a grand piano. The complexity of the cooperation required is geometrically magnified over that of a small ensemble. This is easily recognized by the players. So they yield a great deal of autonomy, nearly all musical freedom, independence, and personal ideas and interpretations of the work to the all-powerful conductor. It is a rational, even an essential decision.

There may be circumstances in other fields of leadership where the complexity of execution is so great and the consequences of the performance so important that we yield similar levels of executive power and personal freedom to the leader. War comes to mind as an example. We certainly give up much personal autonomy when we serve in the armed forces. But even in war, the generals are clearly unable to know everything about the enemy and the battle as it progresses, making battle an improvisation on a theme, rather than a tightly scored work. Therefore, individual initiative among the junior officers and rank and file is encouraged where appropriate. It is never appropriate to encourage this in an orchestra, at least not during the performance.

At the heart of this challenge is the illusion that we can and should control others.

Most of our complex systems require some degree of individual initiative and improvisation if the desired results are to be achieved. And for this reason, among others, our approaches to leadership typically permit, even encourage, a degree of individual creativity and independence among the players, but not in a symphony orchestra.

If the conductor is an extreme example of executive leadership, then the orchestra is also a peculiar example of followership. Each player's considerable gifts, honed by thousands of hours of practice and sacrifice, are surrendered to the control of the conductor. The players have often spent half a lifetime alone with their instruments only to excel by creating ensemble with others. It is a peculiar collaboration, but I can tell you, having played in orchestras as a youth, that it brings a peculiar joy when the orchestra achieves the performance they seek together.

THE CONSEQUENCES OF EXECUTIVE POWER

Given the extreme degree of executive power vested in the conductor, it wouldn't be surprising to find a corresponding degree of arrogance developing in the character of such a successful and celebrated leader. In fact, stories of conductors who have crossed the boundary of personal sanity into megalomania are not at all uncommon. The very way their work is carried out encourages this, if they have a personality at all susceptible to the power they wield. When this occurs, a particular illusion creeps into the vision of the conductor. It is the illusion that *he* is making the music. The absurdity of this is apparent to all but the conductor. Not a note proceeds from the baton, a silent ivory stick that makes no music at all, no matter how passionately the conductor may slash the air with it. Alone, the conductor is capable of nothing. Only when he steps before a willing band of players can his expertise result in beautiful music, or for that matter, any sound at all.

Few leaders may imagine themselves to be working from the metaphor of the symphony orchestra conductor, but the illusion to which he is supremely susceptible is there for many of them, if in less bold relief. It is the illusion of control.

For this reason, it is not uncommon to find a leader in almost any role who thinks the music being produced is *her* work. Many a leader has, quietly and thoughtlessly, made the leap from knowing her role to be leveraged, of significant importance to the work of the whole, to believing she is the source of the work. Here is a form of megalomania that is all too common among leaders, a particular form of the sin of hubris that may not be so much an inherent fault in character as a virus that grows in the fertile medium of the leadership environment where too much is made of leadership and not enough of the collaboration so essential to most enterprises. And this weakness, born precisely of a leader's success and that of her organization, brings with it a number of pathologies for the organization and the leader.

When collaboration isn't welcomed and encouraged, when the power of the leader is supreme, the side effects—the pathologies of power—are especially evident. With these most of us are, unfortunately, quite familiar. The suppression of dissent, in all forms, is deemed necessary. Compliance becomes a central concern to be measured and tracked as a proxy for success and, in the worst cases, loyalty becomes a supreme value. Those who offer alternative perspectives and strategies are disciplined, ridiculed, banished. The leader can become married to a particular vision or strategy to such a degree that its failure can be interpreted only as a failure of execution, even if the vision or strategy is patently wrong.

Worst of all for the leader and his team, a culture of entitlement can develop, and with it, a complex system of dysfunction in which ego supersedes mission, and the leaders become estranged both from the people who actually perform the work and from those their enterprise is designed to serve. It seems likely that this is precisely what happened in a number of major financial institutions a few years ago, leading to the proverbial bursting of the bubble to the immeasurable misery of millions.

Great leaders know that a coercive manner can elicit, at best, compliance.

Also, this kind of "imperial leadership" often leads to key people disengaging from the work while continuing to give an impression of cooperation—that is, they go underground and become passive promoters of the pathology. (I recall a favorite cartoon in the *New Yorker* of ten identical executives around the boardroom table, each pointing to the one to his left . . . no caption needed.) It is important to remember that the much-loathed habit of palace politics can thrive only where there is not just a monarch but also a court of minor lords and ladies, and many pretenders to the throne.

The real villains in the parable of "The Emperor's New Clothes" weren't just the opportunistic merchants and the self-absorbed emperor; the courtiers and the common people were also complicit in his absurdity. Only an innocent little boy whose parents couldn't keep muzzled, one who had nothing to gain from the system, was able to penetrate the thick atmosphere of falsehood. This resulted, of course, in the supreme embarrassment of the emperor and the whole community, and also in the restoration of some degree of health and truth to the kingdom.

SLOW EROSION OF CHARACTER AND RESULTS

This parable is useful, but the truth is that most of the failures that follow this pattern are less dramatic. Usually the emperor isn't found to be totally naked. The strategy and work that proceed from an imperial leadership model, built on a history of necessity and success, more often lead to a gradual failure, a continuing erosion of the quality of leadership and performance, and a gradual decay in the character of the leader. Some organizations persist for years in this model without anyone quite putting a finger on the problem.

The diagnosis is difficult in part because the erosion of performance is slow and because we suffer from a pernicious and persistent myth in the leadership culture of the west that "great institutions are the lengthened shadows of their leaders." The myth persists, in part, because it has such a strong literary source in Ralph Waldo Emerson.

But it also persists because we want to believe it: If we can just get the right leader, all will be well. This lets us off the hook for our responsibility to be better followers, which includes the responsibility to speak up and to lead from the middle of the organization.

Am I seeking genuine commitment from my associates, or deep down do I want only compliance?

We can almost see the cartoon-like image of a tall, impressive, brooding conductor casting his brilliant shadow over a quailing orchestra. Fortunately for us all, this is only a myth and all the more absurd when given an extreme expression, a caricature, as I have done.

At the heart of this challenge is the illusion that we can and should control others, like a conductor controlling the orchestra. This leads to the careless exercise of power, the intolerance of dissent, the loss of humility, the growth of entitlement, the diminishment of commitment, the obsession with compliance, the justification of coercion, and the almost guaranteed erosion of results. Worst of all, for those of us who choose and are chosen to lead, we can become grotesque caricatures of leadership and of ourselves.

SUCCESS AND HUMILITY

This problem is much more difficult to cure than to prevent. The best medicine, the preventive medicine, is for the leader and the organization to take a much more realistic, and therefore much more humble, view of their success in the first place. Consider the conductor. A truly great conductor and her orchestra know some things about making music together that are worth remembering. First, no performance, no matter how great, can guarantee that the next performance will also delight. Each performance requires a presence, focus, and chemistry that is unique to that moment. When this magic occurs, conductor and musicians are as much grateful as proud.

Do I believe in the talent of those I work with, or do I really think I could do their job better than they can?

Also, great performances are born out of an assembly of talent representing years of individual effort to master instruments and repertoire, months of rehearsals to master ensemble, and a common commitment to a particular interpretation of the score. Thus, no performance, no matter how great, can really be attributed so heavily to the skill and vision of the conductor who, by the way, is completely dependent on the original vision and work of someone else, the composer.

Finally, great conductors, like other great leaders, know that a coercive manner can elicit, at best, compliance. Great music performances require more than mere compliance, however. They require commitment, spirit, and inspiration, qualities much more likely to come from a real collaboration. The co-creation, then, of a great performance must bring together the composer's vision, the conductor's interpretation, and the orchestra's commitment to collaborative excellence.

Further, great orchestras often outlive great conductors. A legacy of greatness can be fashioned, not on the eccentricities of a particular leader, but on the deep and developing strengths of the whole enterprise. Here the collaboration of the conductor, the section leaders, and the individual players is vital. And think of all the people off stage who help to assure the hall is properly set, the microphones are properly placed, the lighting contributes to the performance, the tickets are sold and seats are filled, the audience is treated well and is ready for an extraordinary musical experience, and so on. Clearly, the role of the conductor is vital, but genuine and enduring excellence is a product of the whole enterprise of which she is but one part.

So here are a few samples of questions leaders might take into the crucible for reflection:

- Does our work flow best in the metaphor of an orchestra, needing strong executive control, or would it serve better to think of it as a carefully worked out quartet? Or even a jazz improvisation?

- Do I sometimes think I am making the music?
- Who are the unsung collaborators who make our work soar? Am I grateful? Do I express it?
- Am I seeking genuine commitment from my associates, or deep down do I want only compliance?
- Do I believe in the talent of those I work with, or do I really think I could do their job, play their instruments, better than they can?

Warning! When you take these and other questions seriously in your deepest reflections, you may find yourself disillusioned. This is greatly to be desired when the illusion is as potentially unhealthy as the illusion of control.

LISTENING

NOT LISTENING

LISTENING

THE MOST DANGEROUS THING ABOUT COM-
munication is the illusion that it has occurred.
All organizations and all leaders struggle
with communication issues. Every organizational
climate survey I've ever been involved with has
named communication as either the number one or
number two challenge from the employees' and the
management's point of view. Sometimes the problems
are simply a matter of effort, skill, scale, clarity, and
frequency. For these, better communication techniques
can improve the situation. More often, the problem is
structural: silos of activity and information that aren't
able to connect to one another readily, information
generated in one area not shared with another, and
multiple versions of the same information that don't

quite comport. In these cases, the organization has to change before the communication issues can be overcome.

Applying solutions that make use of powerful communication technologies to these problems of technique and structure achieves varying degrees of success. In a digital world, information moves at the speed of light in all directions. Unfortunately, so does misinformation. If we aren't careful, our technical fixes to the communication problem simply increase the rate of miscommunication, especially if we fail to realize that many of our colleagues (myself included) prefer other modes of communication—

The most dangerous thing about communication is the illusion that it has occurred.

say, face to face or a telephone call. I prefer these latter examples largely because there is less spam to sort out and because I receive much of the information I actually use through interpreting and inquiring after nonverbal cues. Also, when someone like me encounters someone who prefers e-mail, who in fact exults in the facile and frequent communication that e-mail, instant messaging, and Twitter (caffeinated e-mail?) can provide, the irritation factor for both of us can be serious. These frequent, brief messages can begin to feel like my adolescent brother poking me in the ribs over and over again in the back seat of a 1965 Buick station wagon without air conditioning on a cross-country family vacation. Meanwhile, my failure to respond promptly to many of the overtures begins to feel to the sender like a cold brush-off, a thoughtless dismissal.

These ordinary communication issues are in play throughout our complex organizations, including families, and I suppose they always will be. They are a durable part of the human landscape and a constant companion to all forms of organization. Not that we shouldn't continue and renew our efforts to improve communication habits, systems, and tools. But I believe we need a different kind of conversation about communication issues. Most of the time, when we focus on communication at work, we are interested in *how* we can do it better or *what* needs to be communicated. Rarely, however, do we probe *why* communication is so important and therefore *what kind* we need to cultivate.

The Deeper Purposes of Communication

Communication, of course, serves many purposes: informing and aligning managers and associates, reducing chaos and surprises, encouraging effort, describing results, identifying problems, and clarifying expectations, for example. At the surface of our work, all these are important objectives for communication. But I have found that leaders can communicate clearly, frequently, and effectively for all these purposes and still miss the mark, still overlook the most important purposes and consequences of good communication.

The most important consequences of authentic communication are such things as a deep sense of connection to one another and to the work, a shared sense of purpose and meaning, confidence and trust in others, a willingness to make sacrifices for one another, and an assurance that we are operating truthfully. These outcomes are all about person-to-person connection within the community of work, connections that are forged over an extended time through communication that goes beyond mere facts. They are not just a by-product but are a primary outcome we seek when building an organization where

Listening, real listening, proceeds from character. It also forms character.

the work really matters. Clearly, newsletters, e-mail blitzes, company blogs, monthly fireside chats, and all-company speeches aren't going to touch these goals meaningfully, though these may be useful enough for their own purposes.

CULTIVATING COMMUNICATION THROUGH LISTENING

The question for me, as a leader, has been how to nurture an environment of communication at work that can lead to deeper connections among one another, the kinds of connections that move us to new levels of performance and sustain us in times of trial. The key to this work isn't what we generally mean by communication. It isn't so much in the information we broadcast to others, or even the symbols, stories, and meaning we attach to the information. The real key is in what we receive from one another, how we listen and are heard. *Listening* is our most vital faculty for this kind of communication, and this is especially true for leaders.

We all know this at some level. We have all experienced others with a special gift for listening, those who are able to focus their entire attention on us, if even for a few moments, when we feel nothing is more important to them than what we have to say at that moment. This creates a connection like almost nothing else can. We are heard, and we know that we are heard.

When I can listen with integrity, especially to things that might be uncomfortable or painful to hear, I can grow.

My roommate in college was one of these people. He listened fully and with deep interest and empathy. Years later, we are still very good friends, and we can conjure up memories and even actual quotes of conversations that were important to us from decades ago. Our connection has endured and will endure almost anything, and when we are together now, the connection is instantaneous and we can pick up just where we left off, even after long passages of time. When we experience this in an associate, it is a delight; when we experience it in a leader, it is powerful. Differences in our roles, layers of organizational bureaucracy, the infrequency of our conversations are all wiped away in a moment of real listening. It's both engaging and liberating in a refreshing and arresting way. We find commonality of purpose and real power in being understood and accepted by the simple act of being heard.

SKILLS OF LISTENING

Years ago, I made a commitment to myself to become a great listener, even though it wasn't a natural gift I had developed from an early age. I worked at it, noticed the habits of those more advanced as listeners, and tried to cultivate them in myself. I even took a course in listening. You may have, too, when such things were more commonly taught. I learned, as you no doubt did, some useful principles and techniques:

- Be still and pay attention;
- Don't think about your reply until you have fully heard and processed what the other is saying;
- Never interrupt;
- Reflect back what you think you are hearing from the speaker in paraphrase and confirm that you got it right;
- Use open body posture, hands up and open, no crossed arms;
- Make and sustain eye contact, and for heaven's sake don't be looking at "the bird on my shoulder";
- Ask leading questions and probe more deeply;

- Don't feel the need to respond immediately, giving the impression that you've heard all this before and already have a dismissive answer;
- Thank the speaker for what she has shared with you;
- Then, and only then, introduce new information or an alternate view to the conversation, and do so with an attitude and tone of inquiry rather than advocacy;
- If the conversation needs a starter, begin with questions, real questions that matter, and be still long enough for the other to reflect and respond, even if the silence begins to get a little uncomfortable;
- Never flatter, since the act of listening itself, if it is genuine, is enough to reinforce the other to share, and flattery never feels true.

There are many other good principles and habits to be cultivated if you want to be a better listener. Most of these can be taught in a few hours and mastered, with effort, in a few weeks or months, if you stick with it. I encourage you to do so.

LISTENING AND CHARACTER

Here, though, is what no one can teach you, what you can't learn in any workshop or course: No one can teach you that the jerk you have to work with, who makes this same stupid speech, in this same meeting, with the same tired complaint every year, might be worth hearing. He might have something you and I need to hear and learn. He might deserve more than just common courtesy (though that is rare enough) and actually have a reason to expect to be taken seriously and heard, if not for what he is saying, then for whatever is behind his words that he isn't ready to reveal without some encouragement. This can't be learned, in the ordinary sense, because it requires humility. And humility, unlike all the tips on listening listed above, isn't a matter of technique, it is *character*.

This, then, brings us back to the crucible, the place where character can be formed or deformed. Listening, real listening, proceeds from character. It also forms character. When I can listen with integrity, especially to things that might be uncomfortable or painful to hear, I can grow. When I can get past the annoyance, defensiveness, threat, and even the need for my position to

Much of what needs to be said is never said.

be understood just long enough to perceive the real human being on the other end of the conversation and to see that she is just like me in many ways, then I can find common ground. Actually, I can find more than common ground. I can find solidarity with another person with whom I do not have to agree and on whom I do not need to dump my opinions and reactions. Sometimes I will hear a truth or a perception of the truth, at least, which will undermine not only my position but my image of myself. These are especially powerful moments for both of us, the beginning of real humility.

A healthy marriage is full of just these kinds of moments. With years of living together behind us, you would think there would be no more illusions left to be maintained. But my vision is never more myopic and distorted than when I look in a mirror. (My wife, in fact, says I am a "rexic" when I look in a mirror: I think I'm thin, but I'm not.) When I listen to my spouse of more than thirty years, I'm bound to be gently disillusioned in the best possible sense; then real growth and understanding are possible for me. The same can be true in any conversation I may have at work.

People don't expect us to be perfect; only we foolishly expect that of ourselves as leaders.

Sometimes, certainly not always, the other party can achieve these things as well. It isn't a condition to my growth and understanding, of course, but it can happen. Some of my truest friends and allies in our work have been people with a complaint who had the courage to share it and, thankfully, were heard. Sometimes their complaints weren't valid, but their feelings were. Sometimes their complaints, or something close to them, were valid, and I was given the opportunity to apologize, accept responsibility, and ask for forgiveness. Nothing heals like a *mea culpa* from a leader when it is genuine. Remember, at these times, they don't expect us to be perfect; only we foolishly expect that of ourselves as leaders.

THE POWER OF BEING HEARD

One reason this is such powerful stuff is the fact, seldom acknowledged, that most people working in our large, complex organizations harbor some feelings of powerlessness, of inefficacy, of marginalization. It is an unavoidable fact of hierarchy and organization for collective effort. People know that in such circumstances they can't make all the decisions they would want for themselves. When they speak their minds and hearts to those they perceive to have power and are genuinely heard, it restores their confidence that they can make a difference and even make a life in the midst of these limitations.

You will appreciate better how powerful this can be if you recognize just how great a gap can grow between the leadership of an organization and the people who actually do the work every day, especially in a large, distributed, complex enterprise. Staff and leadership can experience a deep separation, usually more apparent to the staff than the leadership, in part because leaders are idolized and in part because they are despised. The former may be somewhat less unpleasant for the leader, but both are harmful to a healthy work community. Genuine listening can restore that health, humanizing and grounding both the leaders and followers.

COURAGEOUS CONVERSATIONS

There is another reason to work toward this kind of listening in ourselves and in our organizations. Much of what needs to be said is never said. Our leadership team once had lunch with a poet friend of mine, David Whyte. In addition to being a brilliant poet, David has a powerful practice as an organizational consultant. When asked for his advice to us as leaders, David gave us a great gift that has served us well ever since. He told us he believed that a core function of leaders was to engage the people in the organization in "courageous conversations" about our work. He pointed out the etymology of the word "courageous," from the French, *coeur*, meaning "heart." As leaders, he taught us we needed to bring the issues of heartfelt importance about our work into the work. How many staff meetings have we all attended where there was, as they say, an elephant in the room, something that needed to be said and discussed and that had the power to overturn our mundane discourse on the trivia of our work and get us to *the main thing*? We have learned, over time, to allow those conversations to come up, along with the conflict, discomfort, and fear that can attend them. Sometimes we have to convene these conversations. David, in fact, told us we needed to pay attention to what courageous conversations we weren't having and convene them.

This whole line of thinking can be very important to the progress of the organization and the growth of the leadership. Note that just as hope is indispensable in moving us forward, sometimes despair, in measured quantities, is important, too. It is often the only thing that can move us past self-satisfaction, obsession with comfort and safety, and denial when a real problem is looming. Not only can a courageous conversation raise the unflattering mirror up to a leader for her own good, it can do the same for an entire enterprise.

Two issues are worth some comment here. The first is how a busy senior leader can balance the need to listen authentically to voices and persons throughout the organization and still meet the other demands of the job. I have two suggestions. First, consider this intentional listening a part of your core responsibility, an important part of your daily work, not a distraction. Plan to listen. Schedule opportunities to hear what others think. Be sure your meeting agendas are organized to invite discussion and have time for you to listen. Many agendas are so packed they send a powerful message to every participant that no comment is really welcome, and if the agenda doesn't send the message, the other meeting participants will. Therefore, always have a few important questions handy, real questions that matter to you and to the enterprise, and ask them. And when you encounter others at work, be intentional about giving them your full attention; it isn't usually how long you listen but how well you listen that counts.

> *Deep listening holds out the possibility that we might become something better than we are.*

Whatever your schedule and agenda may say, the person in front of you needs your undivided regard, if only for a moment.

Second, we need new technologies, new approaches to listening in our organizations, ways for more people to be heard and to hear others. Some organizations have experimented with new models of communication that emphasize listening such as high-bandwidth meetings, town halls, interactive blogs, training where meeting facilitators emphasize making meetings matter, and so on. Often, these approaches are adopted in a crisis or during some major change process. But they might also serve us in the ordinary challenges of our work as well.

If we are open to hearing what others have to say to us as persons and as organizations, someone will have the courage to insist on one of these courageous conversations. Listening, really listening, to one another at these times is the lifeblood of leadership. It serves to disillusion us when we need it most because we are living with an illusion of who we are. None of us and none of our enterprises are all that we claim to be. Deep listening holds out the possibility that we might become something better than we are.

Learning to Hear

It's eight long years since
we walked off the hot terror
of the thieves that stole
into my head and squatted
on the side porches of my brain
with their baggage of migraines,
confusion, and wild spinning rides
in my very own bed.
Then we thought the surgery
that took them and the nerve
we shared was a brutal turn,
the lesser of two evils,
a tragic chapter in a story
that had held such promise.
Today we walk the soft river trail,
smell the fresh morning breath of
sycamores shaking off their slumber,
splashing sunlight we can taste
like chilled summer chardonnay.
I watch you chatter and flit
like the eastern bluebirds
that have colonized the park
for another season, and I
wonder how to tell you that
the last echoes of the white noise
of effort have finally died away
and I can hear clearly
the crystalline voice that has always
been in the wind.

Sandy Shugart

Not Listening

A S IMPORTANT AS IT IS TO LISTEN TO VOICES NEAR
and far in our organizations, there are times when
we shouldn't listen, when listening will derail our
work, our growth, and our leadership. These voices are a
natural part of the crucible and will be encountered by
nearly any leader who dares to lead rather than maintain.
They come from the outside, from people in and out of
the organization, and they come from inside, from the
interior dialogue we choose to cultivate as we grow into
maturity as persons and as leaders. Let me explain.

Some years ago, when my life in poetry was still
largely in the closet, a close friend, who is also a very fine
painter, gave me a special gift. It was a book she used
when she taught and encouraged young artists, called
Art and Fear. The book was written by two academics

whose lives are committed to the development of young artists and who, predictably, find great frustration in the number of bright young artists whose work ends when their higher education is completed. So they focused on the process of making and growing into one's art and what causes some to continue making art and growing in their calling and others to quit: how they dealt with fear, a certain kind of fear that artists know all too well.

LEADERSHIP AS ART

My friend's purpose was to encourage me both in the making of art, my poems, and in the sharing of my work. She understood that fear was the stumbling block before me, and her gift hit the mark. The first time I read through the book, however, it spoke to me primarily as a leader, not a poet. Every insight, every bit of counsel these mature artists and teachers had for young artists, resonated with me as a young leader. I still use the book in leadership workshops and continue to discover important parallels between the work of an artist and the work of a leader. Perhaps this isn't such a great surprise.

There are times when we shouldn't listen, when listening will derail our work, our growth, and our leadership.

Both art and leadership involve a mysterious amalgam of technique and inspiration, of having something to say and having the craft to say it compellingly. Both require mastery of a kind of technical skill but go beyond skill to something like significance. Exceptional leaders, like exceptional artists, are not the ones who best follow the rules accepted as the standard of performance in their time; they are the ones whose performance creates the rules, the standards against which a whole generation of leaders may be judged.

The tragedy of leadership, like art, isn't that so many leaders lead ineffectively with poor technique but that they lead with so little inspiration, so little consequence. They attempt so little, risk so little, and therefore achieve so little. The opportunity cost to our organizations, our communities, and our lives is difficult to measure but would be difficult to overestimate. In contrast, we recognize truly gifted leadership in those who attempt much, whether they fully achieve it or not. The leaders who help us get results beyond those we thought possible, who expand our vision of what may be possible, who are willing to risk choosing a direction others know is impossible—these are the leaders we admire most. Those who accept the received orthodoxy of our organizations— "You can't do that." "What if it doesn't work?" "We tried that before; let's not waste time on it again." "We've never done it that way before."—those are our ordinary, pedestrian leaders. They may at some

Both art and leadership involve a mysterious amalgam of technique and inspiration.

level succeed, but they and their work will never pass the "So what?" test.

SUSTAINING CREATIVE LEADERSHIP

Creative leaders needn't be trying to change the world. They should, however, be willing to change the assumptions, habits, perceived limitations, aspirations, and approaches to the work of their enterprise. It isn't how large the work is that makes an artful leader; it's how artfully the work has been done, no matter how small, and whether it matters that the work is done at all.

The authors of *Art and Fear*, I am sure, never knew they were writing a book about good leadership, but many of their lessons for young artists are relevant to leadership. They point out such things as:

- We do not long remember those artists who followed the rules more diligently than anyone else. We remember those who made the art from which the "rules" inevitably flow (p. 95).
- Art made primarily to display technical virtuosity is often beautiful, striking, and elegant . . . and vacant (p. 96).
- Unless your work continually generates new and unresolved issues, there's no reason for your next work to be any different from the last (p. 99).
- Uncertainty is a virtue.

- Conditions are never perfect, sufficient knowledge rarely at hand, key evidence always missing, and support notoriously fickle (p. 19).

To a seasoned leader, all of these quotes, these gems of advice to young artists, ring true for leadership as well. I encourage many young leaders to read this book and reflect on the analogous issues in leadership in their work. As a result, I have enjoyed many fruitful discussions with emerging leaders where we consciously treat our workday issues as artistic and creative challenges necessary to doing good work.

Exceptional leaders, like exceptional artists, are the ones whose performance creates the standards against which a whole generation of leaders may be judged.

These conversations are always rich in metaphor and in personal insight. Many leaders who have felt hidebound and even a little strange find these conversations liberating. They were often asked to lead because of the creative way they approached working with other people to get results and solve problems. But after they are in leadership for just a little while, they find themselves accommodating to a leadership culture in their organization that is anything but creative. Their youth and newness to the role isn't seen as a resource to inject fresh approaches, but a liability to be trained and seasoned out of them. Experienced peers begin teaching them the ropes, subtly reinforcing compliance with the group and organizational norms and dismissing approaches, even ideas, that don't conform. This happens even if the traditional norms are manifestly failing to get results. This is why so many young leaders feel trapped in their new roles rather than invigorated to new and more creative work.

This pattern of drubbing the creativity out of our young promising colleagues is, I'm afraid, well established in the culture. The same friend who gave me the book used to tell me about being a visiting artist in the public schools. When she visited a kindergarten or first grade classroom, she began by asking all of the artists in the room to raise their hands. Nearly every hand was raised. By the third grade, though, hardly any children would dare to raise their hands at her call. Of course, this same thing happens at our places of work, robbing both the enterprise and promising, creative employees of their best work.

Creativity and Self-Doubt

If we're honest as leaders, we may have to admit that this happens in our own interior dialogue as well. The doubts about creative approaches to solving problems and getting results don't all come from outside, do they? We question and doubt ourselves at least as severely as anyone else does. We come from a staff meeting where our passionate argument about a new approach, a different strategy, has swayed the direction of the group and led to a different decision than was planned, and we say a little prayer: "I hope to God that I'm right." All our certainty in the moment of the argument melts into the honest sense of uncertainty and doubt once the decision has been made. At times we hear little voices asking questions like these:

- "Do you really know what you're doing?"
- "Wouldn't it be safer and smarter to do this the proven way?"
- "No one will know the difference if you take the safer path, and who will really care in the long run?"
- "Who are you to lead the group this way?"

Again, the correlation to creative work in the arts is uncanny. Every painter, poet, sculptor, novelist, or filmmaker of note has heard the same voices. The essence of artful work is to make a choice to be safe or to make something new, with no surety that it will be better, but guaranteed to be more risky. In this, the authors of *Art and Fear* were equally clear:

You have a choice between giving your work your best shot and risking that it will not make you happy, or not giving it your best shot—and thereby guaranteeing it will not make you happy. It becomes a choice between certainty and uncertainty. And curiously, uncertainty is the comforting choice (p. 118).

Robert Fritz makes a similar point in his intriguing book on living creatively. He argues that both we and our organizations are generally following paths of least resistance, the habituated approaches to our lives and our work that make us feel safe and require us to expend the least amount of energy to get where we think we're going. He uses an amusing illustration revealing that the strange layout of the roads in old Boston, often remarked by visitors, have their origins not in the mind of some twisted municipal planner, but in the paths established by grazing cows long before the roads were established. But just try to adjust the course of any of these roads and you will encounter a firestorm of resistance. Similarly, it is important for us to know that to get different results in our enterprises and our leadership careers, we may have to change the underlying infrastructure, and this will inevitably excite fear and resistance in the form of many loud voices, external and internal.

> *The leaders who help us get results beyond those we thought possible— these are the leaders we admire most.*

WHEN NOT TO LISTEN

So this, then, is when you *don't listen*—when the voices, some inside your head, some coming clearly from the organization, are all about safety, about your incompetence and presumptuousness, about how it won't really matter in the end, about taking the tried and true path even though the results aren't acceptable.

I hear these voices all the time. Whenever I sit down to write a poem, compose a song, or draft an essay like this, I hear the voices. Whenever I suggest a radically different strategy for our organization, I hear the voices. When I suggest we might partner with someone who has always been a competitor or that we should bet the business on a new strategy that promises breakthrough results, I hear the voices. Sometimes I hear them louder than others. The voices know all my insecurities and doubts, of course, and never fail to call them to mind. But they also know some important truths. They know, as I do, that nothing I have ever done really measured up. They know that I never quite measure up, that the ideals, values, and principles I have been bold enough to make public aren't always true in private. The voices know my deepest sense of failure and shortcoming, and they use it.

Listening is a vital faculty for every creative leader; knowing when not to listen is just as vital.

This, more than anywhere, is where the process of making art has been most useful to me. You see, no poem I ever wrote felt completely finished. No song was ever quite as fine as I imagined or willed it to be. Every work of art falls short in some important ways. But you can't hold a poem or a song hostage until it is perfect. At some point you have to let it go out into the world, imperfect as it is, and you move on to the next one. Every work is an opportunity to learn and find new problems that the next work may address. To paraphrase my wise counselors from *Art and Fear*:

> Performance always falls short of vision, or it wasn't really vision.

Nothing ever quite measures up, including me. I know that on any given day, someone in my organization can approach me with the complaint that I'm not living up to the values we proclaim, that I am not who I say I am. And they will nearly always be right. Fortunately, these singular events are rare, but the possibility of them looms before me. This, too, can be a blessing, fuel for the work, a source of humility and solidarity with all the other well-intentioned, imperfect people who have to suffer with me.

My advice, in these crucible moments, is not to listen to the "white noise of effort." Instead, try to hear again the poetry of the new vision, the music of the new big idea, and the voice of artistic promise through the din of everyday work. Listening is a vital faculty for every creative leader; knowing when not to listen is just as vital.

GETTING A GRIP

LETTING GO

GETTING A GRIP

S OMETIMES VERY GOOD LEADERS DISAPPOINT US. They change, lose momentum, and lose their edge. Whatever the source of fire and passion in their leadership, it becomes hard to sustain, and the people who have shared the work with them suffer confusion, questions of legitimacy, and loss of motivation.

Soon after being appointed president of a fairly large college, I was asked to attend a meeting of the best leaders in our business. It was a sort of think tank, organized by one of the leaders in technology to support our enterprises, to look ahead and imagine the state of the art in our work some decade or two hence. I had no idea why they invited me, a complete unknown and a very young one at that, to a meeting of such distinguished and successful leaders, but when I saw the guest list, I was eager to participate if only to listen to these sages and grow in my own leadership.

The event was held in a world-class resort, confirming my sense that I didn't belong there. On the first evening, we were invited to a small reception. I attended, knowing no one, and was delighted to see in a little cluster on the patio, four of the leaders I most admired in our work. These were the leaders who had defined the cutting edge in our work for the past decade, whose institutions were the best respected and most heavily covered in the trade press, who gave the keynote addresses at our national and international conventions. With mixed delight and expectation, I wandered nonchalantly out onto the terrace and eased my way into a position to overhear their conversation.

Sometimes very good leaders disappoint us. They change, lose momentum, and lose their edge.

By this time, these four men were in the famous cocktail huddle, drinks curled into the crease of wrist raised to shoulder, facing each other from such a short distance that their bellies nearly touched. Clearly, something important was being discussed, so I leaned in. What I heard was…whining: "No one really appreciates us. No one really understands what we've accomplished or sacrificed. No one knows how hard it is to be me."

I was stunned by this all-too-ordinary and human display of self-absorption and self-pity. It wasn't at all what I expected. I was disappointed and a bit disillusioned. I'm sure I judged these men with the harshness and hubris of youth, having caught them at their worst. I know them and respect them all still. At the same time, the truth is that none of their organizations, all once judged by the profession to be among the top five or ten of more than a thousand across the country, would be in that list much longer. All slipped from industry leader to just very solid but not extraordinary institutions in a pretty short time. They had, to twist a phrase, gone from great to good. Were these facts connected?

The Plateau Effect

At two other points in my career, I watched this development in leaders with whom I was close. In both cases, although these leaders were very different from one another, the pattern was clear. Early in their leadership tenures, they were launching major, visionary agendas for change and growth. There was a great spirit of hope and possibility in the work, and they mobilized tremendous support from deep within the organization. Their renewing leadership brought out the best in their immediate staffs and many others deep in the institutions. They stretched themselves to attempt more and accomplish more than they had imagined possible. In both cases, I can remember people referring to these periods as "Camelot experiences," meaning exceptional moments of clarity and accomplishment that are short-lived. And true to form, both began to wind down after about three years of exceptional effort.

Great things had been accomplished, important goals achieved, and a new standard of performance established. These leaders had been successful. And then they rested a bit, or at least that's what they thought they were doing at the time. But these periods of rest became extended periods of maintenance, plateaus in the performance of the organizations. And the motivating power of vision, hope, and mission was replaced with the politics of maintenance: competition within the organization for resources, choices that meant compromise to keep things peaceful, little forward momentum, and a feeling of slowly eroding legitimacy. The moral power of the vision and leadership was waning, its grip and even its truth less apparent in their work. They began to drift. Meanwhile, the leaders seemed tired, distracted, sometimes even depressed. And there was a certain amount of denial in the senior leadership team, a

We run to the familiar. This is the price of expertise, the loss of the innocence of a beginner for whom nothing is familiar and so all choices are still possible.

hopeless attempt to hold on to the spirit they had once had, or to fake it.

Is this a common and predictable pattern? I think we all have seen it. Many of us have experienced it directly, not just as a member of the team, but as the senior leader. It feels like losing your grip, like trying to keep a cheerful song going when the heart for it has passed, like going through the motions and waiting for the old spirit to return. It isn't a crisis. The disease isn't acute; it's chronic. And the prognosis isn't death; it's a slow slide to mediocrity. But having experienced Camelot, accepting less feels like loss and is accompanied by mourning.

Our success makes us comfortable with the way we have done things, and that comfort is what undermines us.

No one and no organization can be in optimal performance mode all the time. Plateaus and rests between peaks are an important part of the life cycle of even the best enterprises and their leaders. The difficulty, however, comes when we seem to get stuck in these periods beyond the time for them to benefit our work and health. We can't be in high gear all the time because the energy costs over the long term are beyond bearing. But the inertia in our organizations and in ourselves can be so great that getting the enterprise moving again after a reasonable pause can also prove very difficult.

THE ADVANTAGE OF BEING A BEGINNER

One more pattern I have noticed is that the peak experiences often occur near the beginning of a new leader's tenure. Is this because Camelot is accompanied by a new king at court, with all the promise and hope for change this may bring? Perhaps this is true, but just as often, a regime change in an organization can be a time of fear, even threat, rather than promise. I believe the reason this often happens early in a leader's tenure is that this marks a time of *crisis* for the organization and the leader. Much is at stake, and everyone is watching. The slate, if not clean, is at least uncluttered. If there are big internal or external obstacles to overcome, the leader is confident, as the new person, that she didn't put them there and can act fairly independently to remove them. A new vision is expected, new possibilities can be explored, the constraints of social obligations are loosened, and realignment of resources is normal at these times. Most importantly, everyone expects change, whether with a sense of hope or of foreboding. And this expectation creates a healthy sense of crisis.

The leader may be full of renewed energy, out-of-the-box thinking, powerfully naïve hypotheses. The ones who succeed are generally humbled enough by the newness of the organization that they are forced to listen and learn, to become something of a beginner again. Being a beginner can be a truly liberating experience. Expectations are fluid, and with rapid learning comes growing confidence and hope. Also, early in the senior leader's tenure, she is aware of a truth that seldom occurs to a junior leader or manager, and that is the genuine possibility of legacy. A new senior leader can be greatly energized by the awareness that every CEO's tenure at the helm *means* something in the end. Like an artist standing before a blank canvas, she knows the first brush strokes need to be bold if the picture is to matter, and this is precisely the kind of crisis we find at the beginning of a new regime. This is why the Camelot experiences are so often, but not always, early in the life of a new leader with that organization.

Causes for the sustained decline from the peak performance periods must be many: physical fatigue; organizational fatigue; being stretched beyond our resources for a long period of time; becoming less open to dissent and challenge precisely because we have invested so much of ourselves in a particular vision; letting our ideas get stale by failing to engage in reflection; and confusing means for ends. But the most powerful cause of this decline is *success*. It is when the burst of creative energy and effort has produced precisely the kind of results we had set out to achieve that we are most at risk of the plateau effect. We have, through hard work, established powerful patterns, some of which will serve us for a lifetime but others that need to be surrendered to the next phase of the work.

Once, when asked about songwriting, the immensely creative Hoagy Carmichael said that when he sat down to compose at the piano, his hands became his enemies because "they ran to the familiar." We also run to the familiar. This is the price of expertise, the loss of the innocence of a beginner for whom nothing is familiar and so all choices are still possible. Our success makes us comfortable with the way we have done things, and that comfort is what undermines us. We become less attentive to the connection between our inner passions and our work, substituting habit for fierce integrity. We begin to deal with the external realities of

Crisis can be a great gift.

our environment and to be guided by them rather than by the insights and commitments that have, up to this point, made our work distinctive. And we stop asking ourselves the hard and interesting questions that we had to ask when we were in crisis.

EMBRACING A SENSE OF CRISIS

This, I think, points to our way out when we feel stuck in between peaks as leaders and enterprises. Crisis can be a great gift. All the opportunities and faculties that attended the crisis of making a new beginning can come together again in a new crisis. I have seen this in my own organizations—hurricanes, state budget cuts, massive technology failures or challenges, massive technology installations, a five-hundred-year flood, and other disasters have served to reawaken our best leadership, to get clarity of purpose and a keen sense of reality, to awaken our deep inner connections to our work, to raise our expectations of ourselves and our colleagues to act out of purpose and not comfort.

The work of management consultant and theorist Robert Quinn has proven helpful to me at times of lost momentum. He and his colleagues recommend revisiting our past experiences of leadership in crisis and remembering what made us effective. And they recommend a series of questions to bring a leader back to her sense of what they call the "fundamental state of leadership," the highly energized and focused leadership condition we often experience in crisis. Their questions essentially reconnect us with a sense of purpose for ourselves and our organizations: What results am I trying to achieve? In addition, and I think most importantly for those of us in the crucible, they ask us to evaluate whether we are "internally directed," responding to our deep desires and wisdom rather than accommodating the politics, social contracts, and external pressures of our roles.

We can, with our leadership teams, intentionally lay aside the baggage we accumulate with success and take a fresh look at our work.

Our best leadership can be reawakened, we can get a grip again on the work we were really made to do, if we go back into the workshop where our best tools were forged and renew them. That workshop is, first, internal. I need to know what I am doing here, what work I've been called to here, and how my deepest sense of mission in the world is connected to the work just ahead of me. This isn't strategic planning; this is personal reflection of the most valuable sort, and it must be done. Second, the workshop is found in returning to the attitude of a beginner, taking a fresh look at everything, creating that best sense of crisis we experienced at the beginning of our leadership assignment. We can, with our leadership teams, intentionally lay aside the baggage we accumulate with success and take a fresh look at our work.

Here is the vital question:

> If we were brand new to the organization today, how would we diagnose its potential and challenges, and to what point on the horizon would we want to sail?

This, too, fits the analogy of being an artist. At some point, no matter how successful a project is, we have to put that canvas down and put a new, blank canvas on the easel. The old work may not be perfect or complete, but it is done. What will the new work mean? What connections will it have to the last work? What problems and assumptions do I need to leave behind to begin this work? How bold will the first strokes be? Creating a positive sense of crisis by choosing to be a beginner again and listening for the clues only beginners are able to hear can give us a renewed grip on our work, even when we think we're losing it.

Lost

Stand still. The trees ahead and bushes beside you
Are not lost. Wherever you are is called Here,
And you must treat it as a powerful stranger,
Must ask permission to know it and be known.
The forest breathes. Listen. It answers,
I have made this place around you,
If you leave it you may come back again, saying Here.
No two trees are the same to Raven.
No two branches are the same to Wren.
If what a tree or a bush does is lost on you,
You are surely lost. Stand still. The forest knows
Where you are. You must let it find you.

David Wagoner
Collected Poems

Letting Go

WHILE GETTING A GRIP IS A COMMON challenge for seasoned leaders, the much more frequent challenge for most leaders and their organizations is letting go. The more common pathology is that of the micromanager. The leader who attempts to do everyone's job is perhaps the most widely experienced phenomenon in organizational life. It strikes me as odd that this should be so common when everyone holds the micromanager in such legendary contempt. Nearly everyone works for this character sometime in her life, yet no one accepts responsibility for being this kind of a leader.

When was the last time you met a manager who walked up to you and said, "Hi. My name is Jane and I'm an inveterate micromanager. I can't wait to tell you how to do your job in every detail." But if you work in a complex bureaucracy of any kind in your life, you are practically guaranteed to encounter just such a manager. What makes this such a universal malady, and what are the consequences for the organization and for the manager with this characteristic habit of leadership? What alternatives are there, and how can a capacity for enabling leadership be cultivated in your own character and embedded in the DNA of your organization?

The leader who attempts to do everyone's job is perhaps the most widely experienced phenomenon in organizational life.

I refer to this as a character trait and not merely a misguided technique because its root is found in the character of both individuals and our culture. For a very long time, we have gotten an important equation backward. We have thought that the trick was to secure

leaders we can trust—certainly a worthwhile objective. But we have so focused on this part of the formula that we have neglected to put a proper emphasis on finding *leaders who can trust us*, the followers. And this is just as important, quite a bit rarer, and very much tougher to discern in those we consider for leadership.

THE LIMITS OF TYPE A LEADERSHIP

I have a friend, a very capable leader from whom I have learned a great deal, who is endowed with what we commonly call a Type A personality. She is hard-wired for intensity, and this is manifested in a prodigious work ethic, a tremendous power for focusing on her goals night and day, and a compulsion for controlling everything in her organization. During many long conversations, she would amaze me with her power to call to mind and express clearly virtually everything her organization was working on. I often felt incompetent during these conversations, lacking the command of the detail of the many projects pursued by people throughout the organization that would bring us to the goals we shared. Then I finally realized that when she had described her institution's work, she was really describing *her* work, carried out under her watchful eye and close coordination by others who had much to contribute but were hamstrung by the need to satisfy her not only with the results she envisioned, but also with compliance to her vision of just how they should get these results. Their own God-given capacity to invent new ways of getting to their shared goals was rarely engaged, and so their capacities for creativity and invention were diminishing even as they were achieving her goals.

The organization was successful but stunted, and their sense of ownership of the work, and therefore their commitment to it, wasn't growing even as they were succeeding. She ran a tight ship, but in the end it was just one ship. I envisioned the work as something more akin to a convoy, a fleet of ships, each guided by a different captain with unique gifts and contributions to offer, each with its own course to set while we all sailed to a common point on the horizon. Everyone knows a fleet has more firepower than one ship.

The consequence for an organization with a domineering leader, no matter how bright he may be, is diminishment. It will accomplish less. There will be fewer unpleasant surprises but also fewer pleasant ones. Many of the serendipitous benefits of a more open organization will never be realized under the dominator. And the capacity, flexibility, nimbleness, and readiness for new challenges in the organization will never grow in such a controlled environment. Like a hothouse plant, the enterprise will not respond well to hardship, will not adapt as well to new conditions as they are experienced, before the leader is even aware of them. Further, many of the most talented members of the team will not flourish in response to the heavy-handed control. Some will defect to find a place where they can be stretched by the opportunity to grow their own gifts and vision. Those who remain for long may actually be damaged by the diminishment of their own gifts and a concomitant loss of confidence in their ability to navigate challenging waters.

> *A leader who can't learn from her team already has an unhealthy relationship with them.*

Risks of the Character of the Heavy Handed Leader

It isn't just the organization that is damaged by such heavy-handed control, however. The dominant leader is also subject to a variety of problems. I recall another senior leader, expressing dissatisfaction with her team's performance, telling me she felt she could do the job of every team member better than they could. It was a shocking comment but an honest one. She really believed this. The consequences of such hubris can be severe. To begin with, she has rendered herself unable to learn from others in the team. And a leader who can't learn from her team already has an unhealthy relationship with them, one that is bound to get worse as resentments grow and trust erodes. At best, her colleagues will refocus their energy on pleasing her rather than achieving excellence in their shared work. (I lie awake at night sometimes with the fear that my team would rather satisfy me than do the right thing. This is the deepest of pathologies that can infect the executive suite, leading ultimately to spectacular failures.) At worst, her team, feeling disregarded and distrusted by their leader, will engage in all manner of behavior worthy of distrust: turf mongering, sabotage, self-interest, pandering, or going underground. This serves only to confirm the leader's hypothesis that the others "just don't get it," and her habits of micromanagement are justified and reinforced, her arrogance growing by the day.

In addition, the burden of the micromanager is the necessity of always having to be right. It is a terrible weight, but he must bear it along with a sense of risk and anxiety heightened by his isolation and exposure to criticism when he is, inevitably, wrong. This sense of risk is often not so unrealistic, as our culture loves the notion of ultimate responsibility and is all too quick to identify the team's failure by quickly replacing the coach with another minor autocrat, avoiding the need for deep transformation of the whole organization. (The connection to professional and collegiate sports here is almost palpable as the musical chairs of head coaching continues at an ever more rapid and expensive pace.) This whole situation turns up the heat, so to speak, in the crucible, making it unbearable and destructive to all but the most resilient souls.

Collaboration requires a sharing of power but not abdication.

COLLABORATION AS A WAY OF LEADING

The alternative to micromanagement is not, as I have occasionally heard, "abandonment to the competence (or incompetence) of others." But it can feel this way if no one has equipped the leadership with a workable alternative. The alternative is, in a word, collaboration. Here is a word often used but seldom given any real definition. It's like jazz. No one can quite define it, but we know it when we see, or rather, hear it.

Collaboration requires a different technique, a new set of tools. It also requires, and forms, a different kind of character in the organization and its members. In a genuine collaboration (like jazz), everyone has a voice, but all voices are not equal. The ground of collaboration is a common purpose, a deep agreement on ends that allows for a wide range of improvisation on means. It is, by nature, experimental, hence the etymological similarity of collaboration to laboratory. It requires a spirit and habit of inquiry in the organization. This is harder to achieve than we might imagine, since almost all of our organizational lives have been suffused with the politics of work where the presumptive approach is advocacy, where constituents come to every decision with interests to be protected.

Improvisational work requires that each player looks for ways to build on the contributions of others.

In fact, the dysfunction of many enterprises that have failed to cultivate a culture of collaboration can be traced to this one defeating habit. A modern university is a good example. Power is in some manner distributed or shared, but the habit of work is advocacy, where participants in the organization come to the decision-making process with minds made up and political skills carefully marshaled toward earning a win for those they represent. The result is gridlock, a rough balance of power (sometimes a balance of terror!) among constituents with adversarial views, masked with a kind of patina of collegiality.

The instrument of destruction is the committee, perfectly designed for conserving what already exists but perhaps the least effective tool of innovation or collaboration ever attempted. The result is an environment of adversarial posturing, competition, turf protection, and moralizing of position where everyone tries to stake out the moral high ground. In such a state, to disagree doesn't make us merely different or even wrong, but somehow disturbed. What for some in the enterprise seems like a necessary move becomes for others an act of coercion. At best, they may comply with the direction for a time, but eventually some are likely to rebel, subvert, or check out.

So pseudo-collaboration, that is, power shared but employing the old tools of command and control, such as advocacy, is a poor solution. It is frequently accompanied by a characteristic question, "How do we get buy-in?"

Here's what I know about "buy-in." On many Saturday mornings, I used to arise early with my son, the youngest of our four children. He loved pancakes and loved to serve them to his mother and sisters. So I got out the pancake mix, measured the ingredients, and put them all in a mixing bowl. He stirred. I heated the pan, applied the oil, poured the batter into the familiar disks, flipped them, and put them on a warm plate. He precariously carried them to the table. When the others had finally dragged themselves to breakfast, he announced, "Dad and I made pancakes!" This is buy-in. It is supremely paternal and utterly appropriate for a nine-year-old boy. It has no place in mature organizational life.

A SHARED THEORY OF WORK

Collaboration requires a sharing of power but not abdication. When I collaborate, I am still in the room; I still have voice; so do the others. To this new environment of shared influence we must bring new tools and attitudes. They are the tools of mature conversation. We seek a rich dialogue informed by data and a spirit of inquiry. We listen deeply and argue in ways that focus on what we think we know and how we know it and on what we think it means. We are seeking a shared theory to explain the data. Reaching substantial agreement on the underlying theory of what is happening is the vital step. Then strategies can be developed, argued, modified, or rejected on the basis of the theory, not on the basis of one's power or flash.

This theory of work, like all theories, is conditional and therefore subject to challenge and revision on the basis of new information or a new way of organizing the data. It requires continuing dialogue and inquiry, even while we execute the strategy. When the strategy comes up short, as most do, the old pathologies of organizational life needn't reassert themselves. No one is to blame; no one's pet project has to be defended; no one need be embarrassed or compelled to spin the facts to avoid embarrassment. We simply go back to the laboratory, revisit our data and theory of work, and refine the strategy or find a new one.

It is the shared theory of work that connects our organizational mission to strategy in rational ways. In fact, a leader can't have a very promising strategy unless it is born out of a theory of work. It also liberates the team members to improvise on the theme, using their creativity and competence to add their unique contributions to the overall work. This is the jazz. To achieve and sustain this kind of creative work requires more of every member of the ensemble. It also requires making room for others to contribute. It makes better players of every member, including the leader. In time, the team develops great facility at just this kind of improvisational art, because they have mastered the disciplines of collaboration. And the results can be powerful. Not every work project requires such a process, but most benefit from the spirit of collaboration because it can produce better decisions, better work.

THE PHILOSOPHER'S STONE

To a more traditional leader, this whole process can seem treacherous and foolish. Why give up power? Won't others take advantage of me if I unilaterally disarm? What if it doesn't work? Aren't they still going to blame me?

This puts the leader right in the middle of the crucible, with its heat, pressure, and reactivity, at least for a time. But there is a philosopher's stone for this crucible, as well, that can bring wisdom and transformation to the process. It is the recognition that the threat the leader feels, her essential vulnerability, is not a weakness. Rather, her very vulnerability is a faculty, a powerful capacity to generate more and better work from the organization by genuinely engaging a broader array of perspectives and gifts, but only if she knows how to let go in a way that enables collaboration. This is not disengagement, but a kind of loosening of the grip more akin to improvisation, just like in jazz. The essential requirement in the conversation that makes improvisation work is captured in the phrase "yes, and…" rather than "no, but…"

Improvisational work requires that each player understand the impossibility of creating anything worthwhile through control. Instead, each player looks for ways to build on the contributions of others. You, the leader, are still in the room, still engaged; you still have voice. But you use your voice in a way very different from advocacy. In fact, contrary to advocacy, where your goal is to undermine the other person's position and compel her to yours, in improvisation you seek to make the other player ever more brilliant with your contribution, with your "yes, and . . ."

Letting go, then, isn't a form of giving up but more a way to give in, to join the creative community on terms no one member completely controls. Not all work requires or even benefits from this kind of collaboration. It isn't an end in itself but a means for producing the best work where collaboration is appropriate. It is most beneficial in the processes of design, of planning and strategy, rather than routine execution. In fact, it greatly eases many of the difficulties of execution by creating just the trust and mutuality that enable people to do their jobs well, rather than someone else telling them how to do those jobs. I have seen this spirit transform organizations and the results those organizations achieve.

It also transforms the leader's experience of the crucible from something like battle or politics to something much more like ensemble, authentic teamwork, jazz. Instead of being exposed and judged and isolated by her role, she can join a community of work, a work of co-creation. She can find mutuality and fellowship in the work. She can learn from all of the other players and share genuine admiration for their competence, letting it complement her own.

> *Micromanagement diminishes both the leader and the led. Collaboration, practiced and perfected, enlarges both.*

Micromanagement diminishes both the leader and the led. Collaboration, practiced and perfected like any other craft, enlarges both, nourishing the underlying conversation that gives all our work meaning. Even to the inveterate micromanager, the promise of collaboration makes a winsome proposition. Who wouldn't trade the role of overseer for a life of making music? I'd call the one who made that choice lucky.

Lucky

There are times I need to pinch myself
to prove this isn't just a dream,
this work that reaches right down
through the rich loam of rhythm and harmony
to the roots of joy and shakes
the whole tree of my existence
with laughter and apprehension that
no matter how hard we play
this can't last.
And, of course, there are times when it
feels like going through the motions.
Not that we're phoning it in, but
there just isn't anything happening.
The notes are all there in the
correct combinations, the right order,
but there's no connection, no groove,
no conversation, no jazz…
But if I keep playing, keep trusting,
even a hollow performance eventually serves
only to intensify the real music,
when it happens. And it will happen
When the planets align, or the gods condescend,
Or the fundamental particles resonate with
The wave of the co-creation
Which is to say
it feels, I feel so incredibly
lucky to be here in the endlessly unfolding work;
So lucky not to be going
through the motions of all the other

jobs and careers and options
to which I might have been resigned;
So lucky to be here with you
who also know the rush when it
all comes together;
So lucky to have learned, the more I practice,
The luckier I get.

Sandy Shugart

FAILURE

FORGIVENESS

FAILURE

☙☙☙

S OME YEARS AGO, WHILE WORKING IN HOUSTON, Texas, I was given a tour of an amazing facility for manufacturing drill bits for the oil industry. No industry is quite like the "awl bidness": capital intensive, full of huge risks and rewards, and at the very edge of developing technology. This factory illustrated all these traits. Oil drilling bits themselves are rather remarkable, comprising spherical plates with hardened nubs that rotate along more than one axis. They can be as small as a softball or as big as an armchair. Since they are lowered into deep holes where they may encounter every kind of rock, soft and hard, as well as intense heat, corrosive chemical solutions, and intense pressures, they are made to exacting specifications. The metallurgy alone involves the very limits of our technical knowledge. Since they are at the bottom end of a drilling string, the bundle of pipes, lines, instrument packages, drilling fluids, and other gadgets and materials that can stretch to thousands of meters in length, the failure of the drill bit is a serious matter. If the bit seizes, the spinning string will wind up like an overused yo-yo, complete with kinks and knots, doing much damage. In addition, the whole string then has to be removed from the drill hole, shutting the operation down for days and costing many thousands of dollars. For all these reasons, oil drilling bits are manufactured to the severest standards and tolerances.

Failure is unavoidable if the work has any real value or takes any risks at all.

The factory we were touring certainly reflected this. We were surrounded by computer-controlled metal-working machines, stocks of the highest grades of steel, a serious community of design engineers with their state-of-the-art CAD systems, quality control technicians, x-ray machines, and so on. As we were leaving the manufacturing area, I noticed an area in one corner of the facility that was marked "FAILURE ANALYSIS." Asking our tour guide what it was, he replied that it was where the smartest folks in the company worked and walked us that way.

Here was even more sophisticated machinery— microscopes, x-ray crystallographs, ultrasonic testers—and on the shelves, many drilling bits that had obviously failed. The head of the Failure Analysis Group then described a variety of tests used to analyze the multitude of ways that bits can fail. We looked at many of them. Some were pitted, others scored, a few looked to have nearly melted, and some had broken into fragments. Justifying such a huge investment in quality control, they explained the essential necessity of understanding how and why the bits failed so they could improve their design and production; so much, after all, is at stake. I asked, then, what percentage of the bits that failed came back for analysis. The answer: one hundred percent. Then I asked what percentage of the bits they manufactured eventually failed. The leader replied, "Oh, all of them fail eventually, and so all of them come back—or what's left of them."

What a difference it would make if we went into our projects understanding that failure is a part of the lifecycle of our work.

I was incredulous. Having toured many factories and worked with all sorts of industries, I couldn't name even one that expected *every* product they shipped to come back. Ultimately, for this company's products, failure was guaranteed; it was in the nature of the work. Every bit was employed in drilling until it failed. Everyone was conditioned to expect failure in every product. But every failure was also an opportunity to learn, to understand what made that product go as far as it did before it failed and how that time and use might be extended. Every failure, then, contributed to the success of the next generation of products—EVERY failure, not just some statistical sampling.

Admittedly, the oil industry is one of extremes: extreme ups and downs; extreme conditions for the extraction and transport of their raw material; extreme technologies; and, at least some of the time, extreme profits. But sometimes the best way to learn a thing is to see it illustrated in the extreme, to see the truth in bolder relief than normally seen. Could this be one of those opportunities?

RESPONDING TO FAILURE

Failure, in most of our organizations, is seen as somehow aberrant. When a product or solution fails, we assume something went wrong and we see it as a problem. Immediately, we go into problem-solving mode to discern how to fix that problem and, if we are especially thoughtful, to solve it at a systems level and assure it doesn't happen again. So far, so good. But often this is accompanied by all sorts of other collateral consequences, especially if the culture of the organization or profile of the leadership is intolerant of failure in the first place. Someone must be to blame. Someone must have dropped the ball. Someone has to be held accountable. The exaggerated collateral consequences, in turn, cascade through the organization in unhealthy ways. Because blame inevitably follows a problem, a lot of energy can be expended to deny the problem exists in the first place. This usually presents as an unassailable bureaucratic defensiveness: "There's no problem."

Once the evidence mounts to such a level that the problem can't be denied, the response shifts from denying the existence of the problem toward denying responsibility for the problem: "There is a problem, yes, but it's not my fault." Now colleagues become threats to one another as the organization looks for someone to hold accountable: "Is this a sales problem, a manufacturing problem, or a fulfillment problem?" In addition to wasting energy and time, these responses tend to confuse the data, to compromise the information we might have collected from a careful analysis of the failure that would improve all our future work.

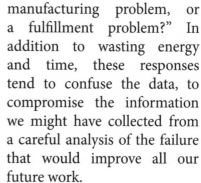

Rather than writing failures off as a waste, we can treat them as potentially rich resources for the next phase of our work.

What a difference it would make if we went into our projects understanding that *failure is a part of the lifecycle of our work: every project, every solution will eventually be obsolete, inadequate, ill adapted to a new reality, or just based on a mistaken notion.* Failure is unavoidable if the work has any real value, takes any risks at all. With this attitude, we can design more boldly, be alert to early signs of failure, act more quickly, and, best of all, learn. Rather than writing failures off as a waste, in which case that is just what they become, we can treat them as potentially rich resources for the next phase of our work. We, too, can develop habits, procedures, and technologies for failure analysis in our organizations that make learning from the work a matter of routine. And much if not all of the collateral foolishness, the emotional and dysfunctional consequences of the old blame-centered model, will disappear.

It may be impractical in some enterprises to analyze every failure this way, although just the thought of it suggests some interesting possibilities: What if every time a student failed to learn there was a serious attempt to determine what went wrong, rather than blaming the student, the teacher, the school, the home, or whatever else we could name to take the blame? To regularly expect things to fail and therefore to require a process of analysis, learning, and improvement might be a significant new source of strength in our organizations, bringing together people from multiple disciplines around a common goal of improvement.

Failure and Organizational Culture

So what has this to do with the leadership and the crucible in which leaders are formed and deformed at work? I want to make two important points here. The first is that at the very core of the work of a leader is the climate and culture of the organization. Within a variety of limits, each leader has some opportunity to help shape and season the environment for the work of others, to create the crucible in which he and his associates work. Therefore, creating this sense that failure is expected, just as success is, and that it is an opportunity for disciplined learning and improvement is leadership work. It requires some courage on the part of the leader to convey this expectation, to suspend judgmental and even visceral reactions when things go wrong in favor of an attitude of serious inquiry and mutual trust. This habit and climate have to be sustained if the culture is to move in the direction we have described, and the leaders in our organizations are uniquely responsible for this.

Just as the Failure Analysis Group had powerful and appropriate technologies available for their analysis of failed drill bits, we may need to invent or adapt technologies of our own. These could be as simple as habits of meeting for careful discussion and inquiry or as complex as full-blown quality-assurance systems. What seems clear is that the tools necessary for learning from failure in manufacturing may be very different from those used in a marketing enterprise or a voluntary association or a public school. That these technologies are sparse outside of highly capitalized private enterprises suggests a lack of both discipline and ownership. It may also reveal a fear of this kind of inquiry because of an ambiguous history of accountability in such organizations. Or it could simply be that certain enterprises find themselves hard to measure. But the emphasis here should be on learning more than measurement—that is, even with imperfect measurement, the process of failure analysis can still be very useful. The leader has a special responsibility to help the organization keep this focus on authentic learning.

The second point is this: leaders fail too. They all make mistakes, choose the wrong strategy, get out-foxed by the competition, miss important opportunities. Individual leaders and leadership groups in every organization regularly fail in these ways and others. If this isn't expected, then the same foolishness that accompanies a failed product can attend a poor decision: denial, defensiveness, shifting blame, and failure to learn from mistakes. Perfection is beyond our reach, yet we act as though it is the only standard for those who lead us and for ourselves as leaders. At its worst, this perfectionism destroys good leaders; at the least, it deprives them of many opportunities to learn and become better.

Confronting our humanity— our frailty, our fears, our frequent failures—is the beginning of real wisdom in leadership and in life.

What if a leader created a climate where mistakes, wrong directions, poor decisions, wrong tactics and strategies, and other ordinary performance issues could be fearlessly named, analyzed, and used as a source of learning? A friend of mine likes to say, "Experience is the name I give to my mistakes." With this habit, clearly practiced by the leader, her own flaws would receive constructive attention, her capacity for better decisions and techniques increased, her performance improved. Why not give the name "experience" to others' mistakes, as well as our own? Perhaps then the team's performance could also improve as their capacity for engaging failure as a learning experience grows under the leader's humble example. Oddly, many leaders acknowledge the need for the team to identify and learn from their errors, but few recognize that this is behavior that must be genuinely modeled. If my expectation for myself is perfection, how can my team choose any other expectation for themselves?

PERSONAL FAILURE

My failures as a leader, however, have not all been technical. The mistakes I have most regretted, in fact, weren't really poor business decisions I've made, but much more personal failures. I have failed others in relationships, failed to live up to their reasonable expectations of me as a person. I've lost my temper, hurt other people, acted or failed to act out of fear, kept information from others for my own purposes, failed to listen, stereotyped, and any number of other failings, each known to myself and some other person. These failures are an important part of the experience of leadership, too. Unfortunately, many leaders resist these as learning experiences and mirror in their personalities the dysfunctions in their organizations: denial, defensiveness, blame. And because these failures feel so public, because leaders often feel such an exaggerated vulnerability, their reactions can be exaggerated as well. This is where the crucible takes on a whole new level of meaning, as we watch a leader melt down in the heat and pressure of public failure and humiliation and sometimes spill her own corrosive reaction on others.

In my experience, it is these very times where failure, my failure, is utterly apparent to everyone. It can be neither hidden nor credibly denied. It is also these times when the possibility of transformation is greatest. Confronting our humanity—our frailty, our fears, our neediness, our dependence on others, our frequent failures, our deep imperfection—is the beginning of real wisdom (the philosopher's stone) in leadership and in life. The crucible, for good or ill, reveals all these things about us to ourselves and to others. How can we respond?

We can take a healthy personal response pattern from the example in the oil business. First, we acknowledge that this kind of failure is a part of living and of leading. It should be expected. It can even be a healthy exercise to discuss failure in advance, to forecast where it is most likely to occur and assess the risk. Second,

Perfection is beyond our reach, yet we act as though it is the only standard for those who lead us and for ourselves as leaders.

we have to make it safe for others and for ourselves to identify the failure and understand it. What are its sources? Is this isolated or is it a pattern? What am I to learn from this that will help me and help us grow?

While a little mea culpa can go a long way here as well, it is essential to move the discussion quickly to the design of future solutions. The point of failure analysis is learning for improved performance, not confession.

Our teams can be of help to us if we have developed the mutuality that enables us to have these conversations with one another, but most important for the leader is that she have a personal system of failure analysis. As a leader, you have to create this for yourself: serious attention to the work you are doing, where you are falling short, and how this is connected to your character. No one can tell you how to do it, but it is there waiting to be done every day. It requires serious reflection and introspection and a fierce honesty with yourself. It takes time and discipline to cultivate these habits of mind and heart.

Are you leading? You will fail. The question is, will it be deforming or transforming?

And it is immensely worth doing, since this is where the long-term impact of the crucible on you as a person is most powerfully determined. If you work at it, you can develop your own technologies for failure analysis. For me, these include questions I revisit regularly:

- What was my biggest goof in the past year and what is it teaching me?

- Have my hopes for my team progressed in the past year, or are we still banging our heads against the same walls? How am I a part of the problem?
- How am I a part of any problem I might identify at work?
- What have I been working on in myself these past six months? Am I seeing progress?
- Would anyone else be able to see the progress?

They also include key people in my life who have both explicit and implicit permission to speak difficult truths to me about myself in the interest of my growth.

Finally, an essential characteristic of this work is a grand sense of humor. Learning from our work isn't meant to be always a painful experience of self-flagellation. Much more often the corrective insight is accompanied by a chuckle or outright laughter. The senior team at a major hospital in our community refers to their blunders as "tuition." By this they mean an investment in learning. And the greater and more costly the tuition, the more important it is to get a return on this investment in the form of learning. This is the kind of environment that makes the analysis possible and the ongoing work of transformation sustainable.

Are you leading? You will fail. Will it be deforming or transforming?

FORGIVENESS

WE HAVE FOUR CHILDREN—THREE DAUGHTERS and a son, our youngest. When Curtis was six, he decided to take up karate. We were all for it, believing it would be a good discipline, teach him a deep respect for teachers and learning new things, and be a lot of fun. Twice a week, we took him to the dojo where his sensei, Barbie, taught the basics to a class of little children. It was great fun, not only for Curtis but also for me and his mother, Jane, who should have an *advanced* belt of her own, having learned everything with him.

After a few months, his teacher suggested he and four other boys were ready to be tested for advancement from white belt to advanced white belt. When the special day came, Curt and his classmates arrived early, pulling a train of parents and grandparents decked out with digital video cameras to record the big moment.

The test was no joke. The children, in this case all boys, though several of their more advanced classmates were girls, were required to demonstrate a number of stances, blocks, and punches on command in Japanese. They recited the first ten principles of karate as taught in the Shotokan Dojo: "There is no first attack in karate..." and so on. They each performed a choreographed set of moves called a "kata." Finally, and much to my surprise, they were required to break a board with a bare fist, in this case a one-inch thick by five-inch wide piece of pine shelf-board.

All of us fail to perform up to job expectations from time to time. But this isn't the kind of failure that requires forgiveness; it requires feedback.

Jane (my wife) and I were accompanied to this event by Kate, our oldest daughter and Curt's twenty-year-old sister, who had been something of a second mother to him as an infant. The three of us exchanged nervous glances, and I was feeling butterflies, as I knew they were.

Another boy, the largest of the five, was asked to go first. We were relieved, but Curtis and the other boys were suitably disappointed and eager for their turn. Sensei Barbie reminded them of the technique they had all learned in practice. She rehearsed it with them in slow motion, reminding them to make a very tight fist, use the heel of the hand, and—most important—hit *through* the board, not *at* it. To emphasize this latter point, she placed each boy's new belt under the board on the floor so that in striking the board they would be reaching beyond the act to the belt, and hitting *through* the board to reach the goal. Then she whispered phrases of encouragement into the boy's ear, revved him up for the deed, and said "now!" The boy struck through the board and it popped in two. No one was more surprised than he. His father did a victory jig, as much because he had caught it all on camera as for the deed itself. The new advanced white belt took his prize and sat down.

Curt was called next, and he leapt at the challenge. So did my stomach. Jane and Kate were white knuckled in their folding arm chairs. Sensei Barbie followed the same drill with Curtis—coaching, slow-motion demonstration, words of challenge and encouragement building to a frenzy, and then the release. He lunged at the board—all forty-four pounds of him. But at the last moment, I saw it, he doubted. He pulled his punch, and though he hit the board hard enough to make a good bruise, it didn't break. My heart stopped; Kate's and Jane's mouths were agape. "Not to worry," said Sensei Barbie. She set him up again—

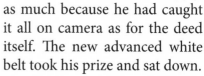

Forgiveness is required for a different kind of failure, the kind that undermines relationship, trust, and mutuality.

coaching, demonstration, words of encouragement (meanwhile I'm making irrational prayers: "God, break the board! Send a thunderbolt!"), and then, "Release!" And again, he pulled his punch. He hit the board, but it didn't break. "Ok," said Barbie, "take a seat," handing him the board.

He was devastated, stunned, humiliated. He took the board and sat down. As his failure dawned on his little boy ego, he was crushed. Covering his face with both hands, he desperately held back the tears and groaned a six-year-old "nooooo..." We were all in agony for him. And the agony was to be prolonged, as three more little boys each went through the drill, each amazed to break his board on the first or second blow.

I looked at Jane and Kate and saw their hurt for Curtis, feeling the heat of his humiliation, the dismay of his disappointment. We were helpless. We couldn't break the board for him, and we couldn't tell him it didn't matter. It mattered to him. I wondered when this would end.

But then Barbie called Curtis back. She took his board and examined it. "I think something's not right with this board. I think it's defective," she said loudly. "Let's get you a good one like the other guys had."

How can I thank Sensei Barbie for knowing how to help him save face? And his face *looked* saved, a combination of relief, joy, and determination. With a new board and a third chance—and more hastily uttered parental prayers—Curt broke this one. The crowd of parents gave him a standing ovation. I got it all on film. Jane and Kate cried a mother's tears of relief.

A few minutes later, Curtis and I were driving home in the big red pickup truck I had brought straight from work, just the two of us. "You know, Dad," he said, "that first board was defective." He kept the second board, the broken one. We'll discuss all of this again, when some future failure looms, as it must for all of us.

Later that night, as I journaled my thoughts about this episode, I had something of an awakening.

Where the practice of forgiveness can help us the most at work is in those situations where someone has failed on the basis of a real error in judgment.

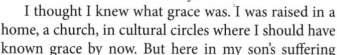

I couldn't break that board for him. I couldn't lower the standards, couldn't minimize the failure. I was a helpless father, but with all my heart I wanted him to break it, not for me or for his karate success, or to avoid the public failure, or for the lesson he would learn from this, or any other obvious reason. I just wanted him to break the board so he could know the taste of a little success and, in his little boy way, someday love himself as much as I loved him. But even more, I discovered, *I had never loved him more than in his moment of defeat and anguish. I had never loved him more than when he failed.*

I thought I knew what grace was. I was raised in a home, a church, in cultural circles where I should have known grace by now. But here in my son's suffering and failure, brief though it was, I was still learning the lessons of grace. In the moment of our failure and defeat, when we feel we least deserve it, that is precisely when we are loved most extravagantly, almost scandalously. In the moment of my disappointment at the failure of another—a family member, a colleague, a role model, a leader, an employee—that is precisely when I am called to love most extravagantly. I can't do the work for them; I can't lower the standards. But I can love them while they fail, struggle to recover their footing, and suffer through the process. My prodigal heart chafes at this truth, but now I know something of a father's perspective on this. And knowing this, I wonder how I can put this discovery, this gift from my six-year-old son, to work in my life as a parent, a husband, a neighbor, a disciple, a leader.

The lesson is one of forgiveness, not the kind of forgiveness we typically practice—"forgive and remember," as a friend of mine says—but the kind of restoring, regenerative forgiveness that can change a life and maybe even the results we get at work.

You won't find this topic in any management book I've ever seen. There's no language for it, no vocabulary that doesn't cause serious discomfort. It's a bit religious, isn't it? It's a bit too personal; can't we keep things on a professional basis? It sounds rigid and moralistic, or soft and new-age, and there's nothing about it in our theories of motivation and employee behavior. Why talk about it at all?

The answer is very simple. Our work involves serious engagement with other human beings. This brings all sorts of issues into play, including psychological, emotional, and spiritual. For good or ill, and usually both, we touch one another, build relationships, encourage each other, and disappoint each other. We are all flawed in important ways, and when you put a lot of us together with tasks, deadlines, decisions, rewards, and reputations at stake, well . . .

ORDINARY FAILURE

All of us fail to perform up to job expectations from time to time. But this isn't the kind of failure that requires forgiveness; it requires feedback and coaching, redirection or reassignment, or in some cases an early exit from the organization. These things happen, more often than not, because of what we call "a poor fit." It isn't a very scientific term, but we know what it is when we see it and sort of know what we mean when we say it. Most often, I find this kind of performance issue is related to a person being asked (or asking herself) to work from her weaknesses rather than her strengths. It is easy to let our assessment of the job or our inevitable comparisons to others guide our work, rather than a deeper understanding of what we can uniquely contribute to the work. For this reason, an important part of maturing in our work is to know ourselves, our gifts and strengths, our deep motivations and what delights us in our work, what we can contribute and how we learn, as well as our weaknesses and blind areas.

Some weaknesses are in areas that can be developed, and they should be; others are more fundamental, and though we may require competence in those areas, excellence may be the wrong goal. Instead, we may be better served by developing our best areas of giftedness, learning how and where to employ these gifts for best collective effect, and partner with others who have such deep gifts in areas where we are merely competent.

Much has been written on these matters of performance that is worth reading. But this kind of failure of performance is not what I want to discuss here, not what really requires forgiveness.

In place of blame, we should put discernment, forgiveness, and restoration.

Forgiveness is required for a different kind of failure, the kind that undermines relationship, trust, and mutuality. Forgiveness is required when people and relationships are hurt somehow. Surely this happens all the time at work. There are ordinary breaches: a bad joke, a thoughtless comment, blindness toward a colleague's need, petty selfishness, and envy. These cause the bumps and bruises we give and receive in all of our relationships, and they require the ordinary, daily forgiveness that all healthy communities regularly practice. It's no big deal but often is overlooked precisely because we are at work. And when it is overlooked, there are cumulative consequences that we recognize: strains, stresses, petty dishonesties, backbiting, sniping, and a host of other foibles that degrade the quality of our community and the quality of our work. For this reason, it is important for the leadership to model this kind of forgiveness, both giving and seeking it. It creates, or rather completes, a climate of courtesy and respect that is essential at every level of the organization. And when the leaders begin to act as though they were somehow exempt from these ordinary virtues, the virtues tend to deteriorate at every level of the organization.

Never underestimate the value of courtesy, or "manners," as management expert Peter Drucker likes to call them, in organizational life. He refers to them as the lubricant for the organizational mechanism. I think they are this and much more. They are a glimpse into the deeper values of the human beings who influence the culture of the organization most powerfully. Deep courtesy indicates deep regard for other human beings; lack of it suggests that people are just a means to an end.

Failure That Undermines Trust

In addition to these ordinary mistakes, there are also egregious breaches, serious failures of character and trust that can create turning points in the life of an organization, and certainly in an individual. These are not as rare as we might think. The headlines that cover great falls from grace by astonishingly overpaid executives touch only the very elevated tip of the proverbial iceberg. Inappropriate relationships, power politics gone mad, ends justifying all manner of means, humiliation of others, theft, lying, cheating, plotting, and scheming—a veritable Shakespearean landscape of human tragedy and comedy can be found at many work places. These are a bit beyond the scope of this essay, however, and what it means to forgive a fallen leader of mythic proportions when there is no evidence of repentance or remorse, and no effort at restitution, is for someone else to record.

Where the practice of forgiveness can help us the most at work, I believe, is in those situations where someone has failed on the basis of a real error in judgment, a failure of character. The failure and the consequences may be manageable or may be very serious. But we're not talking about a mistake, acting on incorrect information or making a poor technical decision or just being a bit offensive toward another person. Where forgiveness is most vital is where the failure raises questions of trust, where the person who has failed is left wondering, "Will they trust me again, or will there always be a shadow over my work, my decisions?"

A brief story will illustrate. Years ago I promoted a person to a leadership role who lacked some depth in the technical part of her job but had the perfect character to build a thriving, trusting, entrepreneurial organization. Many looked askance at the decision because she wasn't judged to

An important part of maturing in our work is to know ourselves, our gifts and strengths, our deep motivations and what delights us in our work.

be the most qualified, based on formal education and experience. (Competence tends to be overrated, if you ask me. It is easy to become competent at most anything, if you need to. Character, the way you are wired together, is the much rarer qualification, and it can't be changed much on the job.) A few weeks after she was hired, a ruckus developed. She had fired a long-time associate of the organization who was now seeking an audience with me for himself and his lawyer. So we all met together, the fired associate, his lawyer, my young leader, our lawyer, and me. As I listened over the course of the next hour, a few things became very clear: the man needed firing, and he was fired for all the right reasons; however, my young leader had overreacted in the moment, and the procedure used to fire him was all wrong, making us quite vulnerable to legal action.

Her mistake at first seemed to be procedural, technical in nature. But the real failure was one of judgment and of character, the need to prove her authority to him and to other onlookers. This may seem a small thing, but it is actually quite serious. When a manager's emotions, especially fear, overwhelm her judgment, and everyone sees it, it is a violation of trust. How will they expect her to respond the next time they encounter a threatening situation? Will they trust her to lead through the issue without caving in to her fear? Will she use her power as a manager wisely? Power and trust are precisely the flaming torches every manager is expected to learn to juggle.

Fortunately, the fired man didn't want his job back but wanted a settlement which, it turned out, was quite modest. Everyone in the room knew that my new leader had made a mess of this firing that was going to cost us. She, most of all, knew this now, and was visibly shaken by the whole matter, her confidence seriously undermined. When the meeting concluded, I asked her and our attorney to remain behind. I'm certain she was expecting a scolding, a lecture, more probing of her judgment. (What were you thinking?) Instead, I wanted to reassure her that this mistake in judgment notwithstanding, she still had my full confidence and trust. She was not to let this issue undermine her growth as a leader, but to learn from it, use it as a point of reflection, and know that it would not cross my mind again. We named her failure, but she was forgiven and restored. She went on to be a very fine leader, delivering all that I had hoped and more. This scenario may not have contributed so much to her success, but it did remove what might have been a serious obstacle so her natural strengths could continue to develop and shine.

DISCERNMENT, FORGIVENESS, RESTORATION

Unfortunately, serious mistakes, failures of judgment, generally get a different kind of treatment: in a word, blame. Figuring out who is responsible when things go wrong is practically an obsession in some organizations. If only they would put as much energy into figuring out who is responsible when things go well and how to replicate that. Blame accomplishes very little. Its purpose is to shift liability from the blamer to the "blamee." Surely the one being blamed generally already knows she has failed. Most of these failures sting so much precisely because they are so public. Rubbing it in isn't accountability; it's venting and posturing. Accountability would be served, perhaps, by working through with the person responsible what she has learned for the future and how we might support others susceptible to this same failure before the fact.

In place of blame, we should put discernment (What is to be learned here about the organization, the work, ourselves?), forgiveness (We all fail, but I still believe in you.), and restoration (Now get back to work and show your real character by your best performance). If the discernment leads to a reassessment of the fit between the person and the job, then it should be addressed thoughtfully, honestly, and discreetly. No purpose is served by further wounding the person. This all requires a kind of fierce honesty tempered with the courtesy that comes of genuinely forgiving the person's failure.

A Leader's Need for Forgiveness

Forgiveness, however, takes on additional dimensions for a senior leader, as I have discovered in the latter part of my career. As a senior leader in a large organization, many decisions no longer come to me. More specifically, staff deeper in the organization, closer to the work, make nearly all of the operating decisions and do most of the problem solving. This means that only certain kinds of problems make it to my level now. All of the win-win choices have already been made by others; the choices between better and best, or between good and bad, win or lose, are largely made by others as well. By the time a decision gets to me for all the right reasons, it is often "lose-lose," a choice between bad alternatives. In many of these, any decision I make will hurt someone. Even neglecting to make a decision, often the path of least resistance, will hurt someone. This has not been an easy adjustment for me.

In fact, it is a hard truth for many to admit. I remember being a participant, years ago, in a very fine leadership development program. All of us in the program were being trained and certified to teach a leadership course to college students. All the other trainees were college faculty members; I had kept from them the fact that I was a college president as long as I could, but it eventually came out. The course made very good use of literature and film to set the stage for discussions of leadership. One evening, we watched "Billy Budd, the Sailor" as a discussion starter. It is an excellent novel and film. You

Deep courtesy indicates deep regard for other human beings; lack of it suggests that people are just a means to an end.

may recall the essential problem in the story. Billy, the cabin boy beloved of all the crew and the captain, is forced to kill the exceptionally cruel first mate, who is justly hated by all. But the iron law of the sea makes this a clear-cut capital offense. The captain, who truly loves

Billy, is then forced to judge and condemn him, and Billy dies at the hands of those who love him.

The course then calls for a discussion of the captain's choice. Was it right? What alternatives could he have employed to solve this problem? How would we as leaders respond to an analogous challenge? Others responded with various plot-altering suggestions. When the time came for me to speak, I took a different tack. The captain did what he had to do; there was no choice. Here is one of the quintessential American naturalistic novels whose central message is the iron law of karma—some problems can't be solved; we are not in control; the best one can do is act in good faith. And from the perspective of a seasoned leader, I could add that many decisions come to me every day where there is no good alternative. You do, sometimes, what must be done with the humility of knowing that you are not in control.

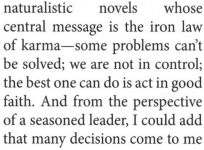

We can be deformed by choosing not to care.

This response created an uproar. Even the trainer was upset with me. Of course, they argued, we are in control. One always has choices. The captain might have done any number of things rather than condemn Billy Budd. Of course, these would have changed the plot, rewritten the story, and missed the entire point of the novel. But my friends in the course couldn't accept, didn't want to believe, that such a situation could really exist in our lives as leaders. I couldn't bring myself to tell them how often this was my reality as a leader.

I have learned the hard way that to do my job well I will often hurt another person, and by extension, the people who love her. Every day I need the forgiveness of the persons I may hurt by even my best decisions. Every day I need the forgiveness of those who care for these persons. And every day I need to forgive myself. If I don't, my only real alternative is to pretend not to care or to learn not to care. And I think not caring is no kind of alternative at all.

Here again, the crucible of our work works on us. We can be deformed by choosing not to care, rejecting the need for forgiveness, shifting the responsibility to the ones we wound, growing tough and calloused. Or we can be formed, even transformed, by forgiving ourselves and others. This is deeply humbling. Forgiving ourselves enlarges our capacity to forgive others. It creates human solidarity with others who have faced hard choices. It makes learners of us rather than judges. In this condition, I find it just possible that the lessons of genuine grace, of loving in the midst of struggle and failure, as taught to me by my son in his karate class, can be applied to others precisely because I know how much I need them to apply the lesson to me.

BEING DETACHED

BEING CONNECTED

BEING DETACHED

EVERAL YEARS AGO, MY FAMILY WAS BLESSED TO BE able to acquire what for us is the perfect mountain retreat near the highest point in southwestern Virginia, a place we can enjoy and give away to others in need of restoration. The charming cabin had a full, unfinished basement, all concrete block and cement floors, which we planned to finish for additional sleeping and living quarters. When the time came, we stumbled into a general contractor who did most of his own work with just one assistant. Before we hired Richard, he urged us to look at his work, which he kept in an online portfolio. I intended to do this but got busy and ended up hiring him without looking. Work soon commenced, nothing fancy, just waterproofing, framing, drywall installation, and so on. As the work began to take shape, we became good friends with Richard, and I eventually did look at his online portfolio. It was amazing. Richard had relocated from Dallas to the hills of Virginia some years earlier, but in Dallas he had been a top-of-the-line craftsman, a cabinetmaker extraordinaire. Multi-million-dollar mansions were graced with custom made libraries, grand staircases, and kitchens designed and crafted in exotic woods by this amazing artist, our friend Richard.

When I saw him next, I gushed over his craftsmanship, which I could clearly see even in the routine job he was doing for us. I apologized to him for the mundane nature of the work we had for him. He smiled and said he was happy to do the work, whatever it was. He knew when he moved to Virginia's mountains he'd have to take the work as it came. "Besides", he said with a wink, "even when I'm hanging sheetrock, I'm still a fine cabinetmaker."

This moment of clarity has stayed with me. Here was a man who had a clear sense of his own identity as a craftsman. It had come from years of labor. Yet, his identity was larger than any particular project he might undertake, and he brought his deep identity to all of his work, no matter how ordinary it might be.

My job isn't me. My career isn't me. My team isn't me. My organization isn't me. This differentiation is vital if the person and the work life are to be healthy.

I have often thought how healthy this kind of connection, and distance, between work and identity can be. Richard has achieved it. He is a craftsman, a fine cabinetmaker, no matter what project he is currently engaged in. He brings his whole self to the work, but the project doesn't define him. He has a healthy detachment from the project, as well as a healthy engagement with it.

Rarely have I seen this healthy engaged detachment so clearly exhibited. Often, however, I have seen the opposite, a tragic overidentification with the work. As I have consulted with scores of colleges and other servant institutions, I have frequently encountered leaders, successful leaders, who are so thoroughly identified with their organizations that they are crippling them. This particular pathology generally comes, not from organizational failure, but from success. Let me explain.

Overidentification with the Organization: Me, Not Me

Among the very first things a baby learns after birth is very fundamental: this is me, that isn't. I call this "me, not me." You can watch the exploration that leads to this differentiation of the child from her environment: touching, tasting, clenching, tossing away, stimulating, looking away and then back again. All of these behaviors help a child to learn the fundamental lesson, what is me and what isn't me. And like many of the earliest lessons in life, this one has to be learned over and over again. Differentiation is an ongoing process.

We notice it at the points of bold relief (I was tempted to call them high points, but some are terribly low) such as the rebellion of a teenager, moving away from home, separating from siblings, separating from children and letting them go, and the death of parents.

I believe this has to be learned at work as well. My job isn't me. My career isn't me. My team isn't me. My organization isn't me. This differentiation is vital if the person and the work life are to be healthy. For leaders, the risks of failing to differentiate are exaggerated. You may feel particular ownership for the enterprise, may even be a founding leader. This heightens the identification. You may experience a much more public sense of exposure and liability for the results of the organization than anyone else precisely because you are the leader. Because our culture tends to overvalue the contribution of the leader to the success of any enterprise, every public success leads others to reinforce your identification with the organization. You may come to feel that because you are the leader you know things about the work that no one else in the organization knows, forgetting that they all know things you don't and perhaps can't know. There are many forces at work to cause the

Leaders who aren't thoughtful when their organizations experience great success or failure run the risk of sliding into confusion over "me, not me."

leader to identify deeply with the organization and its performance.

This can be a healthy thing if the identification is with the purposes, the mission of the organization. Seeing the leader's deep commitment to the mission is important to the followers if the journey they are on together requires them to navigate through any narrow places at all. They can be sure the leader isn't going to cut and run, and so they are more willing to take risks that may put them in that narrow place. If the leader, however, identifies too strongly with the performance of the organization and this is coupled with even a modest tendency to control, things can get strange in a hurry.

Engaged detachment involves differentiation from the organization, and differentiation of the leader's performance from the organization's performance.

In cases like this, the leader takes criticism of any part of the organization or its work personally. She may sulk and pout or she may lash out at the bearer of the criticism. I think virtually every leader feels at least some of this kind of hurt, even from the most legitimate and remote criticism. Interestingly, it is rarely experienced in the first weeks or months of a leader's work with a new enterprise. The identification hasn't occurred yet, so the criticism isn't taken by the leader to be aimed at her. After a few years of hard work, when a leader really cares, the criticism all hurts, at least a little bit. We can react to this pain in one of two ways. We can withdraw, defend, or react in some other instinctive manner: nobody likes pain. Or we can observe the pain, note that we are feeling it, use it as a touchstone to check our reactions and choose to listen thoughtfully. That is, we can choose a kind of engaged detachment, clearly interested in the criticism and how to evaluate it, without letting it get to us personally. Cultivating this kind of connection to the work is essential. But what is meant by engaged detachment?

At its core, engaged detachment involves differentiation from the organization, and differentiation of the leader's performance from the organization's performance. A leader has to be delighted when the organization succeeds but know that it really isn't her success, to be deeply concerned when the organization or someone in it fails but not to take this on as her own failure. This is not abdication of responsibility but a kind of humility before the complexity of our work. Think of a physician who takes both primary responsibility and a fierce interest in the best possible treatment of a patient and her disease, but can't afford to assume ultimate responsibility for the outcome. She shares in the outcome, but doesn't own it fully as her own. If she did, she would run the risk of being paralyzed by every failure, every death, or alternately becoming intolerably arrogant with every success. In either case, her capacity to heal in the future would be diminished, not enlarged.

The Risk of Alienation

Leaders who aren't thoughtful when their organizations experience great success or failure run the risk of sliding into confusion over "me, not me." If their reaction is significant, perhaps even punishing to those bearing the message of criticism, the messengers stop coming. Nobody wants to be the "designated spear-catcher." Thus, at the highest levels around the overidentified leader, a vacuum of information forms, a dissent-free zone in which truly serious mistakes can be made. The leader's overidentification has, ironically, cut her off from the organization. You can be certain, also, that the repressed criticism in the inner circle isn't so easily repressed in the larger organization. Critics abound in every organization. Even if hearing some of this is painful, wouldn't it be better for the organization if you knew what people were thinking?

At the same time this is occurring, in another of life's ironies, the undifferentiated leader has cut herself off not only from information but from relationships with the people around her. Relationships where candor isn't valued become strained, artificial. Genuine friendship and regard is undermined. Over time, overidentification actually brings the leader to a place of loneliness and isolation. Encounters with the staff have a strained familiarity but little intimacy. People are careful, rather than carefree, hoping not to step on any land mines. As professionals, they accommodate the leader's habits, focus on how much they can get done. But the journey has lost something important, and both the leader's and the team's growth is stunted.

OVERIDENTIFICATION WITH PERFORMANCE

In addition to overidentification with the organization, however, there is an even more subtle challenge for many, especially those most gifted and passionate about accomplishing more, and that is overidentification with one's own performance. In this pathology, a person's passion to perform becomes a serious liability to the extent that it becomes more important than the work itself. Another brief story will help to illuminate this.

I once knew two musicians, both extremely talented and hardworking. Both were inflamed with a passion to play and perform at the highest level. One made it; the other changed careers. The difference between them, I believe, was one of how they were wired and how they identified with their musicianship. The one who made it was able to endure almost any criticism, of which there is never a shortage, especially among rival musicians. In fact, she sought out the criticism, exposed herself at every opportunity,

The real tragedy isn't that some have attempted much and failed, but that most have attempted so little and been satisfied with modest success.

and listened with interest and without defense to what others had to say, weighing and filtering what she heard, but rarely reacting or defending. For her, the criticism was fuel for the next seven-hour practice session.

The other was equally gifted and just as driven to achieve excellence, but fragile. Criticism of her work wounded her precisely because she cared so deeply. As a result, she avoided criticism, was too deeply hurt by it to receive, evaluate, filter, and use it. Even mild correction put her on the verge of tears. In the end, the price of improvement was too great for her and she wisely set her music aside to pursue another direction.

It is our identification with limited success that most constrains our possibilities.

The difference between these two is more than just how thick- or thin-skinned each was. It is an issue of identity. One was able to take the criticism as a potential gift because, though she was deeply engaged with all her passion in her music, she was able to achieve a level of detachment from each performance. For her, every performance was prologue to the next and the next and the next.

Leaders in our organizations who aren't able to differentiate from their personal performance can become intolerably demanding of themselves and others, perfectionists who raise the stakes so high on any issue touching their work that few can afford to collaborate with them and none dare give feedback that could improve performance. In the end, they may be so defeated by the issue of "me, not me" that they give up and their talent is lost to the field.

Where the leader is mindful, however, the issues of "me, not me" are a source of great strength. With proper differentiation from the organization and work, a leader and team can surrender ownership of habits, strategies, values, and policies that no longer serve the purposes of the enterprise, even if they were once essential to its success. The organization's and the leader's history of success and failure becomes prologue to future accomplishments without being a ball and chain because they aren't overidentified with these approaches. This opens the leadership to opportunities to completely reconceptualize the work from time to time in ways that their very success might otherwise undermine.

Awareness of "me, not me" can also become a great faculty for understanding the chemistry of the organization. When a mature leader feels a strong reaction to criticism of some aspect of the organization, she can step back not only to evaluate and learn from the specific criticism, but also to evaluate her reaction and what it may be telling her about herself and the enterprise: Why did that hurt me or make me so angry? What does this tell me about the way I am engaging the work now? Is this an indication that others may be avoiding telling me something I need to hear for fear of my reaction? Am I reacting strongly because I disagree with the criticism or precisely because I know on some level it is true?

In this way, leaders have often discovered truths about themselves and their work that have proven invaluable and enabled them to change in response to new realities in the work. Further, avoiding the strong reactions that come from overidentified leaders, cultivating the habit of humble reflection in these times, invites the whole leadership team to be free and engaged and mature. I can't begin to tell you how much more satisfying and healthy that is for the entire enterprise.

JOB AND WORK

One further insight into this healthy engaged detachment: When a leader looks at her job as a project, one of many she will engage as a craftsman over the trajectory of her career, it gives her a very valuable perspective. The crucible of work can exaggerate the importance of issues that really matter less than those involved can imagine in the moment, leading to an intolerable perfectionism. Seeing each job as a project lowers the stakes to a healthier level. It can be especially helpful in dealing with one of the most difficult decisions for any leader: When is it time to move on? If her whole identity is tied up in a particular job, the leader is often the last to know that a new leader with different gifts

> *Do the goals we have set for ourselves matter enough to make serious sacrifices?*

is needed, much to her humiliation and to the damage of the organization she serves. But if this is just one project that she as a craftsman will undertake among many, she can take a much more sober and realistic view, choosing to recognize when someone else's gifts may serve the organization better and hers might be of better use somewhere else on some other project. In this way, every job becomes a vessel for her work, and the vessel, though important, can be expendable in the interest of the work.

Fundamentally, I suspect more leaders and organizations fail to accomplish all they might because of the limiting effect of success rather than the obvious costs of failure. The real tragedy isn't that some have attempted much and failed but that most have attempted so little and been so satisfied with modest success. It is our identification with limited success that most constrains our possibilities. The maturity that comes from differentiation at work enables us to step back to imagine and pursue significance at a quantum level greater than we have yet experienced. With this comes a new kind of freedom—the freedom of mature work where neither the leader nor his colleagues are under the tyranny of immaturity caused by not knowing the secret of "me, not me."

Breakfast on the Road

While I linger at the corner table
Savoring the last of the lukewarm coffee
Dark and sweet as the Miami night that
Only just surrendered to the morning
Feeling no great compulsion to any activity
My neighbor lands in a rush of readiness
Luggage, newspapers, all-American breakfast in hand
Half perched on the seat, ready to spring, at what signal?
He whips his oatmeal into alertness
Downs juice like a shot
Prowling the paper, shooting caffeine
Scanning the crowd, sizing up
The other predators
Stretching before the wilderness of work
Then he's gone
Almost before he could leave an impression
In the seat
Only crumbs and hastily paid bill remain
To track his passing
And I, still watching from my dish-cluttered blind
Eye the indifferent staff who wonder
When the table will turn

Sandy Shugart

BEING CONNECTED

*"The most important thing for your success is sincerity.
Once you can fake that, you've got it made."*

T HIS PUNCH LINE TO A VERY OLD JOKE STILL MAKES its point. But today I would substitute for the word "sincerity" the much overused word "passion." Passion for our work is the least understood, and most often referenced, characteristic of great organizations and leaders. It has, in fact, become so hackneyed, the mere use of the word is almost a guaranteed turn-off with any audience. I recommend avoiding it at every opportunity. Yet, there is something of vital importance here. Here we find the flip side of engaged detachment, the healthy and sustainable way for a leader to identify with his organization.

A DIFFERENT KIND OF FOLLOWER

Much has been written over the past decade or two of the changing social contract between workers and the organizations (and leaders) they work for. We've seen two decades or more of furious mergers and acquisitions followed by nearly a decade of economic uncertainty. And every transaction was followed by reorganization, down-sizing, cost-cutting—creating efficiencies that are a necessary part of surviving in the marketplace. Globalization has fundamentally changed the relationships of suppliers to producers, producers to distributers, and distributers to retailers. Seismic changes in some industries, such as automobile production, rock not only the industry but also the regions, communities, and families that once were the bedrock of production, where generations of a family worked for the same company.

Passion for our work is the least understood, and most often referenced, characteristic of great organizations and leaders.

Some of the largest sectors of our economy, such as healthcare, are well known for the instability of their business model, the unpredictability of their finances, their shifting regulatory burden and legal environment, and their volatile labor market dynamics. No wonder the social contract has changed. Employers have found it necessary to treat the people who invest their talent and labor in the enterprise as interchangeable, dispensable, temporary overhead. Workers know what the corporate code means when words like "off-shoring" and "right-sizing" are used. Is it any wonder that they seem less committed?

Meanwhile, a new generation of workers has arrived on the scene. However they might be labeled, they bring a somewhat different set of perceptions and aspirations to their careers. For many, the old paternal substructure of employment, the implicit contract so well described by Peter Block in his classic book *Stewardship*, i.e. "you take care of me and my need for long-term security and I promise a modicum of compliance and at least the illusion of loyalty," has been exchanged for a different set of expectations. What many now want are immediate rewards, mobility and variety, rapid advancement, more autonomy, and a much swifter cycle of performance, recognition, and promotion. And to get these things, they are much more willing to move from organization to organization with dizzying frequency.

Is my work worthy of my sense of purpose, or is it really just a means to an end, a step on my personal ladder of success?

Given these developments, it really isn't very surprising that followers look to their leaders with something of a jaundiced eye, especially since all of the characteristics mentioned above are seen most clearly in the leaders. Look at how rapidly the executive suite turns over, how ambitious for the next new assignment, the new beginning, many are, and how little enduring commitment is shown for the long, steady follow-through. No wonder our followers, if they give us any thought at all, harbor deep suspicions concerning our motives and what our leadership may mean for them now and long after we have moved on to the next assignment or organization.

These changes, I hasten to add, are unlikely to be reversed and are not entirely a bad thing. The emerging model of employee engagement promises to be less paternal and to enhance the mobility and the personal responsibility of workers at every level. They create an environment that encourages and rewards flexibility, breadth of knowledge and skill, and a high degree of self-management—all good things. And in the inevitable shortages of skilled workers that our demographics are guaranteed to produce over the next decade or two, this situation may well produce unprecedented opportunity for people traditionally relegated to the economic sidelines, if they are able and willing to secure the education and cultural orientation to navigate the new economy and workplace.

Finding a New Model of Engagement

At the same time, these changes create real challenges for the development of communities of work that seek to achieve significant results over the long term. As leaders and followers both swirl through organizations every few years, there is little time for them to engage in the deep learning, both of the whole enterprise and of its various local expressions, that leads to wisdom in strategy and execution. It is more difficult to build positive culture intentionally and to create any continuity in that culture, a vacuum that is most often filled with a negative culture of indifference, or worse, resentment, cynicism, and demoralization. Most distressingly, the people with whom we work can become objects, resources, tools to be used and disposed of as the company pursues its goals—an approach that may yield short-term gains to the bottom line but almost never leads to exceptional performance over the long term.

I'm not suggesting a return to some older, better model of engagement of employee and organization, follower and leader. The evolution of these relationships is unlikely to be reversible, and we've already agreed that there are some important opportunities for growth in the new models. What I am suggesting is that the new environment places a premium on leaders who can find authentic ways of engaging their organizations and their own work within them. That is what it means in the new context to be "all in." Therefore, I want to suggest four areas of serious reflection and inquiry, if you will forgive me, four "P's," that are useful for anyone's work, and especially for a leader's. They are purpose, persistence, passion, and personal engagement.

PURPOSE

The idea of discerning and pursuing purpose in life and work must resonate powerfully with many people, as several books over the past few years have addressed this question to eager reading audiences of many millions.

In addition to persons, it is a question of extreme importance to healthy organizations, and one easily given only cursory attention. After all, the mission of many organizations is apparent in the business model, isn't it? And let's face it, few really enjoy or take seriously the writing or rewriting of mission statements as a first step in developing the next iteration of the five-year strategic plan. Yet, when we strip away the jargon of planning and the pompous language, the question of purpose is vital to the community of work. What difference are we, uniquely, trying to make in the world? It doesn't have to be life changing;

Followers have a legitimate need to genuinely know their leaders, both their minds and their hearts, to know where their deepest commitments lie.

not every organization will have a mission like feeding the hungry or saving the whales.

The value of clarifying purpose isn't just to assert significance but to claim a clear direction and a value against which to measure it. Sometimes that value is a matter of legacy, the creation of something that lasts, like a great institution. Sometimes it is a matter of service, impact on the world or a community, or the families that consume our product or service. Still other times, the value is a matter of craft, to be the best at what we do and to redefine what excellence means in our endeavor. Whatever the value, clarifying the purpose of the enterprise gives other people a way to connect their purposes to ours, and vice versa, a connection that is all the more important when it may not be all that long-lived. As a leader, you must be able to articulate the purpose of your enterprise in terms that are engaging to those you would like to invest in it, including your followers. And if they have had some voice in shaping that purpose, you will find this connection much easier to make.

Just as important, however, is the leader's sense of purpose and its connection with the purpose of the organization. They will not be the same, generally, but they need to be congruent.

- What difference am I trying to make in the world? And how does my daily work contribute to this?
- Am I doing work that is genuinely mine when I go to work every day, or am I acting, posing, playing a role that really doesn't fit me so well?
- Worse, is my daily work at odds with my deep sense of purpose?

- Is my work worthy of my sense of purpose, or is it really just a means to an end, a step on my personal ladder of success?

These questions are worth asking of ourselves. And don't forget that at some level, our followers will be asking them about us, especially in the new working environment, a new kind of crucible, described above. If we are no longer in the work for life, our followers need to know we are in it for real, and so do we.

PERSISTENCE

Because our tenures with our organizations are tending toward the brief, the question of persistence is becoming more important for leaders and followers alike. This often manifests itself in the hiring process where the unasked question, lingering just below the surface of the interview, is how long the candidate is willing to commit to the work for which he is being considered, especially if the role is in senior

Do the goals we have set for ourselves matter enough to make serious sacrifices?

leadership. Boards of directors have developed more and more sophisticated compensation models to incent persistence in their senior staffs. Often referred to as "golden handcuffs," these models attempt to substitute financial incentives for more organic connections to the work, a symptom of the new market realities in the emerging social contract. Whether these approaches really engage the leaders or not, they serve to highlight the importance our organizations have had to place on the value of persistence.

If, however, the issue of purpose is dealt with both by the organization and the worker, the connection to the work is inherently stickier, more likely to result in intrinsic commitment to persist than any monetary rewards. This is vital to the organization because the commitment we seek to elicit from staff must be modeled by the leadership if it is to endure at all. Why should any worker stretch himself and sacrifice for an organization or a leader who is always open to a better offer, whether the work has reached a modicum of completion or not?

To this end, I find it very helpful for leaders to weigh this question proactively, well in advance of making a commitment to serve the ends of any organization. The question isn't just whether we are a good fit, but whether we find sufficient congruence for our own deep purposes in the world to make a commitment to the organization's purposes. Ask questions like:

- What work am I here to do?
- How long is it likely to take to make the contribution I am being asked to make, and am I willing to see it through to completion?

And later in our tenures:

- Am I still challenged by the work?

- Does it call forth my best and stretch me in ways that will keep me vital and growing?

These and similar questions have proven very helpful to me as I have navigated the questions of where my work might take me. After eight years of intense commitment to the work of a fine organization, one I might have stayed with to retirement, I awoke one night with a certain conviction that it was time for me to move on, not because I was unhappy or disinterested, but because I had completed much of what I believed was my best work and had begun to feel like I was swimming in the shallow end of the pool. And one thing of which I was certain was that I was made for the deep end.

One further thought. As I age and gain perspective on my own life, I feel certain that when I look back across the trajectory of my whole working life, I will value much more highly whether I accomplished anything worthwhile and completed anything that really mattered than I will care whether I took every opportunity for promotion and advancement that came along. With any luck at all, one lesson we will all take from the crucible of our work is to take the long view on our own choices and to look for meaning over reward.

PASSION

I asserted earlier that the much used word "passion" is widely misunderstood. What most mean when they use it is "enthusiasm," or having an excitement or positive spirit. Enthusiasm is a good thing. We can be enthusiastic about many things: a new relationship, a planned trip, our favorite sport, and many elements of our work. They may well take our breath away. What passion means, however, is much more than this. The root of the word in Latin is passire, which means to suffer, as in the unfathomable sacrifice of suffering in the Passion of Christ. Many things evoke enthusiasm in me for which I am not particularly willing to suffer. Here is a question that is much more difficult and valuable to entertain:

- For what am I willing to suffer and sacrifice?

How many couples do you know who would benefit from asking this question concerning their relationship, discerning in the process that what they thought was passion was really just enthusiasm?

This question can be clarifying for our work, as well, both corporate and personal.

- Do the goals we have set for ourselves matter enough to make serious sacrifices?
- Here is a question that ought to be asked in every serious strategic planning retreat. If our goals don't call on us to make sacrifices as leaders, how likely are they to sustain sacrificial effort from anyone else in the organization? Here is what our followers want to know, what they'd really like to ask when we roll out the next five-year plan: What sacrifices will you make?

This is a question I need to ask more often as well. The crucible of work, the heat and pressure and reactivity, is unavoidable; I will experience it. When I do, will the deep purposes I share with the organization, the intersection of my purposes in the world and the organization's purposes, be important enough to me to evoke genuine passion, a willingness to sacrifice and suffer for them? This may be the cure for the scourge of entitlement that marks the executive suites of so many enterprises. Are we ready to sacrifice? Are we "all in"?

PERSONAL

The test of leadership for the followers is much more personal than we often admit. If we are going to lead through any real difficulty, navigate any rough seas, the led need assurance that we are ready to see them through, won't abandon them for an easier or more lucrative gig. And since this is such a deep personal matter, how will they know unless we are in some ways patently transparent? For many, this is a very difficult demand to accept.

> *One lesson we will all take from the crucible of our work is to take the long view on our own choices and to look for meaning over reward.*

Quite some time ago, I counseled a relatively new senior vice president of a very good college. He was brilliant, committed, witty, attractive, good on his feet; in short, he had all the gifts that should be required for a successful chief academic officer of a college. Within three years he had moved on to a presidency of his own, but with unresolved and conflicted feelings about his tenure. About a year and a half into his vice presidency, he asked an important question. Noting that he spent much more time with the faculty than his boss, he wondered how it was that they continued to push back against his leadership efforts while they seemed more than willing to follow the president wherever he suggested they might go together. Was this a matter of the president having been there longer? Was it a matter of the CEO's position in the organization vis-à-vis the president's? Was it a question of charisma? The answer to all of these questions is, "No."

Leaders must continually ask: is my work worthy of my sense of purpose, or just a means to an end?

My good associate had yet to realize that what followers want from their leaders in an organization like this isn't just their cleverness and best ideas, not just their work ethic and willingness to get down into the trenches, not even their charisma or vision, if we are blessed with any. What followers want, in the end, is them. They have a legitimate need to genuinely know their leaders, both their minds and their hearts, to know where their deepest commitments lie and how they relate to their shared work. My associate, for all his gifts, was the most private man I had ever met, charming and clever, but opaque. He could expect their regard and respect for the gifts he brought to the work, but they were unlikely to follow him anywhere really challenging or risky in the end. The faculty of his college shared a deep, abiding sense of purpose, as did their president. What they needed to know and couldn't discern was whether this vice president really had more than enthusiasm and drive for the work, whether his purposes in the world and in his work were deeply congruent with theirs, whether he was likely to persist, and whether he was ready to sacrifice, even suffer for the work with them. In the end, they couldn't discern whether he was "all in."

Despair

Hope

DESPAIR

Endurance comes from enduring.
~ Rainier Maria Rilke

SEVERAL YEARS AGO, THOSE OF US WHO LIVE IN Florida were visited by three uninvited guests. In a period of just over a month, three hurricanes made their way across the middle of the peninsula we call home. First came Charlie, a fast-moving and powerful wind storm that caused much structural damage in the few hours it took to traverse the state. On its heels came Frances, a huge, ponderously slow storm we thought would never leave. Finally, Jeanne visited a combination of high winds and constant heavy rain on communities that hadn't begun to clean up and recover from the first two cyclones.

As each storm approached, we all watched the news closely with mixed fear and fascination, and prepared as best we could for the potential damage, the loss of services, and the interruption of our normal lives and work. Television reporters did their best to sensationalize each event, filming in the now ridiculous idiom of the stalwart journalist, suitably dressed in emergency gear as the wind blew debris and surf and driving rain past the cameras. Some neighbors braved the crowded evacuation routes and emergency shelters. Most stayed home and hunkered down.

Leaders can't afford to be fatalistic. It is in the nature of the perfect storm that no one knows if it is survivable. But surrendering to the fear and stress guarantees it isn't.

I was struck at the time by the way the media covered the storms. Everyone seemed to personalize the weather, not just naming the storms, but ascribing emotions and motives to them,

as though a powerful and dangerous stranger was visiting us. "Charlie bears down on central Florida!" "Frances has Orlando in her sights!" "Jeanne overstays her welcome." It was as though we could handle the threat so long as we could name it, find a way to relate to it, perhaps even reason with it. The storms, of course, have no personality, no intentions whatsoever. They are simply physics, the way wind and water behave under certain conditions prevalent during certain seasons in the southern Atlantic Ocean. But you can't negotiate with physics, you can merely try to predict, accommodate, and endure the plain physical facts. Such a thing unnerves us because it reminds us of how little control we really have over our lives. And we want control.

This is true of our work lives as well. We want to sustain the belief that we are generally in control. As

In strong organizations, people don't just work there—they belong.

⸻ 🔥 ⸻

long as we don't do anything really stupid, we imagine, we can achieve in our work a kind of equilibrium that enables us to predict our future, plan accordingly, and enjoy the fruits of our labors. Without such assumptions, it would be difficult to sustain our constant efforts to plan, set goals, and work to achieve them. Most of the time, the hypothesis works reasonably well, and things are manageable.

Sometimes, though, we are confronted with the awful truth that there are powerful variables, essential circumstances that are far beyond our control. Global financial conditions, major disasters, unanticipated shifts in the cost and supply of energy, political upheaval, any number of circumstances can introduce chaos into our work and lives, creating sustained stress, unavoidable failure, and even despair. Any realistic theory of work has to account for the possibility of such things, and leaders would be well served to prepare themselves for the possibility of what has quickly come to be known as "the perfect storm," after the book and film of that title. (Notice how quickly some metaphors enter our workday lexicon. It is usually evidence of how powerfully the image organizes the data of our experience, how true it rings to a large number of people.)

THE PERFECT STORM: CONDITIONS OF SUSTAINED STRESS

A perfect storm is more than the ordinary storms we are expected to navigate our enterprises through on a regular basis. It is the rare confluence of a number of remarkable challenges, immense threats, any one of which could sink us, as they come together to form one long, sustained, overwhelming threat. We don't overcome such a storm or defeat it; we merely endure and survive. Think of how the Great Depression and the Dust Bowl combined in the 1930s to create an event as threatening to our way of life and as important to the formation of the character of a generation as any world war. From our distance in time, we see the overall picture of this immense economic storm, as if from a weather satellite. But what must it have been like to navigate this as a small business person, a farmer, CEO of a manufacturer, head of a hospital, or governor of a state?

Today, we see the '30s as a crisis that had a beginning, a middle, and an end; they experienced it without knowing if or when it would ever finally relent. Such a disaster may seem remote, but the more recent

Great Recession has brought into focus the very real possibility that any of us may find ourselves struggling to keep our enterprises from being swamped and sunk by such a tempest. So we would do well to contemplate how to handle the sustained threat, exhaustion, fear, and other challenges we may face as leaders. Some of this is technical in nature and peculiar to the kind of enterprise we lead.

The college I serve has, like most, endured several years of serious state budget reductions combined with unprecedented enrollment growth, a product of the recession. To be sure, we have used a variety of financial and other strategies to weather a very long storm and continue to do our best work. But it isn't the development of these technical strategies that has tested us and rewarded us the most in these trying circumstances. The real battle is deeper, more about our spirit than our spreadsheets.

The perfect-storm experience is, first, an experience of sustained fear and stress. So what else is new? Many of us have lived and worked under sustained stress for years. We have come to think this is normal, the way things just naturally have to be. We work in an environment of stress—to perform, to compete and win, to meet sometimes ambiguous expectations, to do more with less. Fear can be an almost permanent feature in our lives. We may work for a manager who is much worse than difficult and incompetent, but is cruel. We may work in an organization that is so dysfunctional that everyone in it has reason to fear. Then we come home to the evening news. Enough said. We turn away from the news to entertainment that is violent, threatening, and disaster laden. We may think this is normal. A perfect storm raises our already chronic levels of stress and anxiety to much more acute levels.

HEALTH AND STRESS

It is important to note that we were not made for this. Our bodies are not adapted to an environment of sustained stress. For the many years that preceded the past few hundred, human beings were carefully and precisely adapted to an environment of relative peace— hunting, gathering, and much more recently, cultivating— interrupted by rare moments of acute stress—say, the threat of a saber-toothed tiger. Our bodies know this. The basic physiology of humans is designed for very rare episodes of fight or flight, those infrequent occasions where we need extraordinary energy, strength, and focus in order to survive. So under this short-lived stress, hormones are

When we lead from principles, followers can be sure of who we are and how we will lead no matter what comes at us.

pumping, energy is being produced very quickly, fat is being stored, blood pressures spike, pulses race, and so on. Does this sound like a staff meeting to you? Even in times of normal challenge, we experience emotions at work and beyond that exact a heavy cost on our basic physiology.

We have manufactured an environment in modern life that creates, almost unavoidably, a situation of chronic stress, and our bodies are reacting to it as though it were acute. The health problems we experience as a result are well cataloged: high blood pressure, heart disease, diabetes, stroke, auto-immune dysfunctions, you name it. When we encounter a perfect-storm situation, this is magnified greatly. Now the stress and fear really are acute but with no end in sight. At some level, we may despair of our survival, or at least any predictable future.

No leader wants to appear incompetent or uninformed, so when she doesn't have answers, it is easy to go silent.

Is it possible that our organizations also experience a kind of physiological reaction to a perfect storm of challenges? When a combination of major surprises undermines our best work and our sense of control over our future as an organization, don't things tend to get wacky, unhealthy, disturbing? Especially if this goes on for a long period of time? The particular pathologies of organizational life associated with these circumstances are also well known. First there is a kind of denial, an ungrounded hope that this will just pass or that we can find a quick fix and get everything back to normal. Then there is defensiveness, a desire to circle the wagons and hold on, refusing to adapt or change. Eventually there may be serious fragmentation and alienation, loss of confidence, loss of community, loss of trust, loss of purpose, loss of identity. For the leaders of the enterprise, these are periods of tremendous challenge and stress.

How do we hold the organization together, focus on mission, sort through what changes we can make and act on them? How do we endure the storm? The questions are real. Some storms can't be endured. In these cases, everyone has to learn to live with the loss and move on. But the leaders can't afford to be fatalistic. It is in the nature of the perfect storm that no one knows if it is survivable. But surrendering to the fear and stress guarantees it isn't.

PRINCIPLES FOR ENDURING THE STORM

So what principles can be put into practice to weather the storm? How can our work and our organizations endure such challenges? Here are four principles, sea anchors, if you will. They won't defeat the storm, but they give the organization some stability and the possibility of navigating even the heaviest seas.

Community

A fundamental principle for dealing with hardship is, "We're all in this together." It has to be spoken and acted out. The underlying idea is that all enterprises are made up, not of resources, but of persons. Organizations that have discovered how to connect on a personal level with every member will be resilient. Those that have used people as resources will not. Unfortunately, this isn't a principle you can begin to implement in times of trouble. The groundwork has to have been laid far in advance. In strong organizations, people don't just work there; they belong. But even organizations where belonging is normally a high value will be sorely tested by a perfect storm. The community has to be maintained, nourished, and celebrated. Rituals and symbols long established will be especially valuable when the chips are down. But the work isn't merely symbolic.

When people are under stress, everything signifies. The leaders must practice a fierce integrity during these times. Every decision will tell their staffs what they really care about. For example, taking executive bonuses while cutting staff tells the employees and the customers all they need to know. No amount of symbolic kumbaya can overcome this act of self-interest.

Oddly, sometimes the community of work can be at its very best when under stress. There is something about the way humans are made that calls us together when we are threatened, if the community is authentic to begin with. A crisis can bring us together, though it is harder to sustain when we can see no end to the trouble. But even if we can't, this is a time for authentic community building. If we can't give the enterprise a plan we can guarantee, we can give them ourselves, and this is often enough.

Knowledge is Power

Uncertainty is the hallmark of a perfect storm. With uncertainty comes a feeling of powerlessness that can lead to despair. The best antidote for this pervasive feeling is knowledge. The temptation is to hunker down, a habit that creates isolation in the organization. No leader wants to appear incompetent or uninformed, so when she doesn't have answers, it is easy to go silent. But this is precisely when more information is essential.

Transparency, no matter how vulnerable it may make you feel, is a strength. It is vital that the organization knows everything you know, no matter how incomplete your knowledge. The facts must all be on the table. Absent the facts, the organization will invent its own. Rumors will find fertile soil in which to grow. Speculation and unfounded hypotheses will seem plausible to many in the absence of any other information. In addition, sharing all that you know keeps the organization and its leadership honest, resistant to delusion and denial. It opens up the conversation to alternate hypotheses and new ideas for navigating the storm. It prevents the development of paternal habits that diminish the mutual ownership of the enterprise that needs to be felt deep in the organization.

> *Transparency, no matter how vulnerable it may make you feel, is a strength.*

Knowledge of the situation empowers people to do what they can to improve it, and empowerment (admittedly an overused word) is precisely what they need. Despair's strongest weapon is helplessness. Nothing is more alienating to organizational life. We may think that sharing the gloomy news will depress folks, but the truth is, just like naming and tracking the approaching hurricanes, it gives them some kind of handle on what's happening. Rather than dwelling in anxiety over whether anybody understands what's going on, it frees them to get on with their work knowing that the leaders are engaged, if not fully in control, that someone is at the helm and dealing with reality, and that they are trusted to do what they can to make matters better.

Despair's strongest weapon is helplessness. Nothing is more alienating to organizational life.

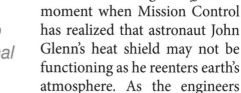

There is a wonderful scene in the film *The Right Stuff* at the moment when Mission Control has realized that astronaut John Glenn's heat shield may not be functioning as he reenters earth's atmosphere. As the engineers debate whether telling him this fact would serve any purpose since he can do nothing about it, the flight controller responds with great conviction, "He's a pilot. We tell him the condition of his ship." Our employees are adults. Whatever we may think of their capacity to react, we owe them the same information we would want to have. It is likely they are going to know it anyway. As my friend says of our organization, "Information doesn't leak around here, it squirts!" Without complete candor, we are unlikely to sustain trust, even if we come through the storm successfully.

Lead from Principles

Even when no one in the enterprise can be sure of what may happen to us, when we lead from principles, they can be sure of who we are, how we will lead no matter what comes at us. They know this best if we are careful to articulate throughout the storm the principles that will guide our decisions. Many leaders take these for granted and assume that everyone should intuit how they will lead. But sustained stress and despair can rob us of this confidence. Be plain. Be clear about the specific values by which every decision will be tested. When the crucible is at full boil, the transforming wisdom, the philosopher's stone, is complete integrity to our principles.

Many leaders think they are trusted with authority because of the results they have been able to produce. This is only partially true. Trust depends much more on how they get results. Naming the principles clearly has the beneficial effect of creating a discipline for the leadership that they may need to avoid acting foolishly out of fear and losing the confidence of the followers.

ORGANIZATIONS AS ORGANISMS

Under stress, organizations sometimes behave very much like organisms. That is, they may behave in ways that seem important for their survival even at the expense of their missions and values. Survival is a powerful motivation for institutions as well as individuals, and both experience the fight-or-flight phenomenon. Sometimes this means paralysis before the threat. I have experienced this myself when suddenly encountering a bear, in one case, and a wild boar in another while hiking alone in a very remote wilderness. Don't organizations experience weak knees, indecision, and wide-eyed wonder when confronted by certain threats? On the other hand, a more common reaction to an obvious danger is bizarre communication and frantic activity aimed at escape or defense against the threat, the organizational equivalent to a blood-curdling scream. In this environment, leaders have a special vocation. They must help the organization keep its wits by attending carefully to its machinery, its almost mindless habits, processes, and procedures, and assure that they are functioning with integrity. Here again I use this word with a peculiar meaning.

Integrity means "connectedness," or "wholeness." The way the organization behaves, and those who may lead it, should have a clear connection to our deepest purposes and values, even when, especially when under duress. Without constant attention, organizations can behave in many thoughtless and sometimes destructive ways. Rules that make sense in normal times might need to be waived for unusual times. Habits that make sense in calm water may be counterproductive in heavy seas. Most importantly, the exercise of power in extreme circumstances can have many unintended consequences, and power is by design unevenly distributed. The leader will be wise to pay careful attention to the effects of decisions on those who are most vulnerable, who have the least influence in the organization. They may be employees far from the executive suite or even clients the organization was designed to serve. The point is, they are most at risk, and therefore we owe them the most careful consideration.

The way we treat the least powerful among us will convey volumes to all the others who are watching and evaluating what our leadership may mean for them. Importantly, in an atmosphere of continuing threat, it is likely no one else will be paying attention to those who need our regard the most.

None of these principles will guarantee the success of the organization, if by success we mean its continuation in the same form and function after the crisis. They are health-giving habits, though, and may enhance the chances for survival and success. This much seems clear to me: the conditions we have been discussing put everyone in the enterprise right in the middle of the crucible—remember the heat, pressure, reactivity, corrosive by-products—both the leaders

> *The way we treat the least powerful among us will convey volumes to all the others who are watching and evaluating what our leadership may mean for them.*

and the led. The potential for serious deformation of their characters, relationships, work life, and purposes in the world is greatly heightened. If the organization comes through the prolonged crisis more or less intact but with deeply mangled characters, what's the point and what may the future hold for the work? If it doesn't survive the storm, then the leaders and followers will be challenged to begin again somewhere else. Will they bring with them the strength of having acted with integrity and courage, or will they add to the burden of letting go of the old organization the wounds of having compromised their characters in the process?

On the other hand, it just may be possible, with the right principles, to navigate even the worst storm in a way that enhances trust, strengthens character, deepens relationships, clarifies purpose, and increases confidence in the work. We have a choice. It takes a little faith. And as others have noted, "faith is just the choice of the nobler hypothesis."

HOPE

A FRIEND AND ADVISOR OF MINE IS MARRIED TO A gifted gardener, a woman with much more than just a green thumb. She has, with his brawny assistance, transformed a large, overgrown lot, essentially a pine barren characteristic of the southern coastal plain, to an amazing, lush, constantly blooming delight. He told me a story once that has stayed with me. It seems his wife had him plant a remote corner of their yard with rather plain seedlings of a bush with which he wasn't familiar. He prepared a bed, planted, mulched, and watered. At the conclusion of his labors, it looked little different to him than when he began. And so it was for the next couple of years. But, three years later, the corner was an explosion of color, a breath-taking addition to their landscape. My friend expressed his amazement to his wife. "How did you know," he asked, "that it would look like this three years later?" She replied good-naturedly, "This is why you will never really be a gardener, honey. You see, from the day I had you plant it, I've always seen it this way."

This is a story of hope and transformation. What was a barren corner in the landscape was seen clearly as a place of extraordinary beauty from the very beginning of the project. Realizing this potential required both technical expertise and a serious investment of sweat. But the real catalyst to transformation was a special kind of hope, the kind that intuits the extraordinary potential laden in ordinary circumstances and can see the transformation from the beginning of the work.

Hope is the conviction that what is happening means something, the struggle matters, the sacrifice and the sweat and the risk have value.

I sometimes wonder if the metaphor of a garden wouldn't help us in our work more than the more common images of competitive team sports. We can win by barely outperforming the competition on any given day, a victory that may last a very short time. But a great garden is a transformation, realizing the best we can get from the land, and one that can endure and flourish for a long time, making a contribution not only to the gardener, but to all who behold and enjoy its fruits.

Hope as an Agent of Transformation

So what might the story of hope and transformation be in our everyday workplaces? For some, it is creating results that no one ever imagined possible. I have been involved in just such a transformation of a college for more than a decade—gardening takes time and patience—with results that are setting a new standard in the industry. This is a "good-to-great" story, as the college has always been very solid, but now has a chance at genuine transformation as an organization and an opportunity to help lead the transformation of an entire industry.

Other transformational stories are more back-from-the-brink to new greatness. One that received a lot of attention some years ago was the complete transformation of Continental Airlines from "worst to first," as one book so well described it. I remember Continental Airlines in the early 1990s, when it was failing, chaotic, desperately unhealthy. I was living in north Houston at the time. Many of my friends went to work there as though they were at a vigil at the deathbed of a patient attended by wacky doctors still practicing leech craft. The end was just a matter of time, and management was a constant comedy of errors. Then Gordon Bethune and Greg Brenneman were brought in to attempt to

Deep integrity in our work speaks to the connectedness of who we are to what we do.

save the company. Many things changed: the strategy became rational; employees were listened to and given a real stake in the company's future; trust was restored; quality of service was put back into the center of the mission; new meaningful metrics were shared widely; and mindless bureaucracy was diminished. Still, the real difference I noticed among my friends, in just a matter of months, as the airline went from worst to first, was renewed hope.

The people who made Continental perform every day began to believe the airline had a real future, not just a chance to survive, but a chance to be great. They believed that what they did mattered, what "we" were trying to accomplish had meaning. The return of Continental was about the return of hope, and hope, in turn, produced motivation at every level.

Sometimes I think we have overworked poor Maslow and his hierarchy of needs in our theories of organizational development. For two generations we have accepted a motivation theory, or its caricature, that requires people to be safe and secure before they can be asked to undertake really challenging work, the kind that is inherently risky, deeply demanding, and moved by vision. Safety and security, we have thought, are essential preconditions to our willingness to serve others, engage our creativity, defer rewards, and endure challenges for some future outcome. Before we can ask those we lead to share generously, collaborate selflessly, bring their passion to bear on their work, we have believed we must assure them of physical safety and some measure of material comfort. I'm not sure

Maslow said exactly this, but he is commonly thought to have done so.

There is, of course, much evidence to support the essential hierarchy of needs described in Maslow's hypothesis on motivation. Much modern organizational theory accepts this work as axiomatic. On the other hand, isn't there powerful data to suggest that people often act courageously, passionately, creatively, and selflessly precisely when safety and comfort, even survival, is least assured? Some of the best artistic work has been born out of the worst circumstances of poverty and insecurity. Indeed, the image of the starving artist is legendary to us. Many of the noblest stories of human service begin with a choice to reject comfort and security, to put one's own survival at risk to serve others.

The leader becomes something of a storyteller, a weaver of the myriad details into a coherent narrative, one that hangs together and affirms our underlying beliefs about the meaning of the work.

But perhaps most importantly, Maslow's theory is essentially personal, that is psychological and individual, and therefore unable to account for much of our lives, including our lives at work. This is because much of what we experience is social and spiritual in nature, as well as personal. And this is where hope plays such an important role, since it transcends the personal and the communal. In fact, it knits the two together.

Hope is an inner assurance that a better future is possible, if not for me, then for someone for whom I deeply care. It is the belief that something I may be able to do could make a difference. Most of all, it is the conviction that what is happening means something, the struggle matters, the sacrifice and the sweat and the risk have value. With hope, all our other human faculties are awakened, all other motivations become possible. Mere survival and safety are poor proxies for real hope.

I'm not arguing that we should ignore Maslow and be unconcerned with the safety and comfort of our colleagues, or even with the more prosaic "aligning incentives to outcomes." But while we do so, let's not fool ourselves into believing that this is sufficient to produce good work. For some, in fact, it can lead to complacency and laziness. If we take our work seriously, or more accurately, if we take our communities of work seriously, then we have to recognize hope as an essential part of the organizational climate. It is the spiritual dimension of our enterprise that we can't afford to ignore but have so little vocabulary to discuss. Nevertheless, I believe many of the important turnarounds and breakthroughs in business have been about hope.

BRINGING GENUINE HOPE TO WORK

What kinds of leaders bring hope to their organizations? How is a sense of authentic hope nurtured in the pragmatic rough and tumble of daily work life? I want to suggest three or four characteristics of leadership that nourish hope, though I'm sure there are many more.

Entheos

Robert K. Greenleaf, the man who first coined the phrase "servant leader," wrote of these leaders that they possessed a quality he called "entheos." He chose this word from the ancient Greek to capture the notion of one who gives "sustaining spirit" to an organization. This idea is easily misunderstood, however. Our culture has a fascination with leaders that borders on idolatry. We elevate them to the level of the heroic and are surprised to discover that they almost never measure up to the myth we, and sometimes they, have manufactured. A part of this hero worship is an unsavory fascination with the details of their lives. Like adolescent fans of some rock star, we are genuinely interested in what they think, say, wear, and buy. The infamous question, "Boxers or briefs?" wasn't really asked out of irony, was it? This foolishness comes with a motto discussed earlier that is desperately misguided, in spite of its literary origins (Emerson): "Great institutions are the lengthened shadows of their leaders."

Followers can forgive anything but a lack of purpose.

This is not "entheos;" this is ego. We have had enough of ego-centered leadership.

By contrast, consider clear examples of deep servant leadership, such as Nelson Mandela, Elie Wiesel, and perhaps the best known example in the world, Mother Teresa. She founded a worldwide movement, the Sisters of Mercy, that has brought healing and comfort to millions. Her legacy as a leader is incalculable. Yet, what do we really know of her personally? Most people know next to nothing except the mission to which she gave her life—comforting the poor and the dying. Most know that Nelson Mandela spent decades in prison because of his deep integrity that led eventually to a bloodless revolution in South Africa, overturning apartheid, one of the genuine miracles of the twentieth century. Few know anything of his personal life, his unmatched courtesy even to his opponents, his deep and genuine forgiveness toward President F. W de Klerk, with whom he negotiated this miracle.

Many know Wiesel's powerful book, *Night*, but few know the courage and sacrifice required to revisit his horrific past in Auschwitz and write a nine-hundred-page memoir that was later abridged into the shorter but no less powerful work. This is entheos. Perhaps less famous, but also extraordinary, is a friend, CEO of one of the most successful furniture manufacturers in the world, who for decades has chosen to be paid a fraction of what his peers command because he believes in principle that he should not earn more than seven times the salary of the least paid of his employees. This, too, is entheos.

We need leaders who will identify deeply with the mission, the abiding higher purpose of our institutions, and will take care to protect their role from the perverting effects of ego-pandering. Leaders with entheos bring hope and engage others to give themselves to the mission as well.

MAKING SENSE OF THE WORK

Second, leaders and organizations that nurture hope make sense of their work. This may seem foolish to those who think the meaning of the work is self-evident, but they may be confusing having a clear mission or purpose with the many nuances of meaning that arise for us and others in our work. Even when the mission is clear, there is a sense in which the pattern, the dance, the meaning isn't apparent to everyone and at all times. Some seem to have a gift for discerning and communicating what things mean. This is not manipulation, not myth-making with a purpose. It is not, emphatically, spin.

What I'm talking about here are the leaders and organizations that have developed a sense of perspective. They know their own story and can share it. The story is rooted fiercely in the truth and grounded in the real values of the work that is shared. Their decisions are made in the context of the larger story, and their communication within the work community helps others make the connections. This gift, this habit of being gives our work much of its meaning. It takes the question, "Why?" as seriously as it does, "What?"

and, "How?" And the gift of story is that it entrusts that sense-making conversation to everyone.

INTEGRITY AS A SOURCE OF HOPE

A third vital source of hope in our work is integrity. Here is a word that is rapidly losing the fullness of its meaning. The root of the word is botanical. It means connectedness. But to what is our work to be connected?

Authentic leadership connects us in two directions. The first is to self. Deep integrity in our work speaks to the connectedness of who we are to what we do. We have all felt this from time to time, where what we do flows from inner resources, from our true selves. It is where the inner story of who we are and who we are becoming flows into our daily work. This is not quite the same thing as what is referred to in the management literature as "alignment," where the work of the leader is to position the work and the people in the organization so their values, skills, and natural strengths are congruent with their tasks. It is a worthy intention. But I think true integrity in our work is something more organic. It arises from serious reflection, real knowledge of our own emerging story,

> *Nothing destroys hope faster than a sense of powerlessness; nothing nourishes hope better than a sense of personal efficacy.*

as individuals and as a community of work. It grows as the realization of the truth of the work grows. It bears the fruit of deep satisfaction when the work is good and inescapable dissatisfaction with anything less than good work. Here the work of the leader isn't so much aligning people and organization as enabling the ongoing dialogue between self and work, one story informing the other. It can't be forced any more than a plant can be to produce the results we want; it can only be cultivated with patience and a faith in the natural processes behind it.

Also vital to this is the integrity of the leader herself. Again, not just her honesty and trustworthiness, though they are indispensable, but the connectedness of her inner and outer work. It is who she is and not just what she does that matters, and whether her commitment to the work is genuine, not just that she genuinely seeks the outcomes we declare, but whether this is genuinely her work. In this sense, the deep sense of calling to the work isn't just her personal business, but the business of all who throw in with her. They want, legitimately, to know if she is all in, or if the work is just a means to an end, a stepping stone in her path to success. Greenleaf called this the "unlimited liability" of the leader for the work and the work community.

There is a particular kind of leadership work to be done here, since the connectedness of integrity also refers to the reality of the link between the story of the enterprise and the work to be done. Is this our work? Where does it fit in the story of our collective endeavors? Are we doing this for the right reasons, deeply rooted in the real values of the enterprise, or is it a reaction to something else—our fears, our greed, our competitive nature? To assure this, the leader becomes something of a storyteller, a weaver of the myriad details into a coherent narrative, one that hangs together and affirms our underlying beliefs about the meaning of the work. And for the story to be true, it must be emerging from the work itself, not from the ego of the leader. This means it is constantly in revision, able to be shaped by a continuing dialogue between the work and the co-creators of the work, open to revision and confession of error and misdirection, able to grasp criticism as an opportunity to rectify the work and assure its truth.

HOPE AND PURPOSE

Finally, hope requires purpose. A friend of mine, a very effective leader, once said of followers, "They can forgive anything but a lack of purpose." Collective effort, enduring co-creation is best nourished, not by complete agreement on the details, or even the goals and objectives. In fact, effective long-term effort requires dissent. It is like the rudder of the ship, using friction to keep the course true. But that course, the place on the horizon to which we are sailing together, is defined by shared purpose. If we can agree on purpose, then all the dissent on intermediate objectives and means becomes not an obstacle to be overcome, but a rudder we can employ to guide and steer the enterprise.

Viewed this way, dissent becomes highly valued in the organization. Practiced faithfully, people throughout the enterprise begin to discover their own voices and the confidence that they have some modicum of power, a means to effectively shape the work and their own contribution to it. Nothing destroys hope faster than a sense of powerlessness; nothing nourishes hope better than a sense of personal efficacy. I can make a difference; we can make a difference. And this is the fertile ground in which hope always grows.

Notice that these examples of hope-bringing characteristics are not techniques, not strategies. They are character traits, a part of the deep identity of a person and sometimes an organization, which raises the question, "Can they be learned, can they be cultivated?" The answer is, "Yes, but..." While skills, processes, competencies, knowledge, and even expertise can be developed, with effort rather quickly, character is another matter. It changes, but at a glacial rate, and too often without specific intention. For this reason, as I mentioned before, I place a much higher value on discerning the character of leaders than just their typical qualifications. Most will pick up the technical content of the role, almost none develop the right character after hiring if it was lacking before.

By character, here, I don't really mean their moral dispositions, although that is a part of what we pay attention to in choosing who to follow. More than this, I mean the way the person is wired, how she is made to engage the world and her work. For example, it may be important to know if the person is a natural "servant," to use Greenleaf's language; that is, if the person's natural character is to focus on others rather than self. If not, this is not a characteristic she will develop quickly on the job.

Am I saying, then, that good leaders are born, not made? No, but neither are they trained. Rather, these kinds of hope-giving leaders are formed, usually by deep reflection on experience, both positive and negative. And here is a bit of good news: perhaps the best place for this formation is in the intense heat, pressure, and reactivity of the crucible. It seems that the deep architecture of our characters, though subject to change, is normally rather crystallized. But under experiences of intense emotion, whether duress or joy, our characters and what we believe about ourselves and the world become somewhat malleable and therefore subject to change. This is exactly how so many of our fellow workers' characters become deformed and twisted at work. But it can also be where formation toward desirable ends can occur.

We need leaders who will identify deeply with the mission, the abiding higher purpose of our institutions, and will take care to protect their role from the perverting effects of ego-pandering.

The secret ingredient, the philosopher's stone, the wisdom that makes the difference in our character over the long term, is intentionality. To make of our experiences in the crucible the fuel for our own transformation, we choose to engage our deep architecture intentionally in disciplined, consistent, purposeful reflection on our work and ourselves. There are no short cuts, no how to's. You just do the interior work. And out of this may emerge a character marked by entheos, sense-making, integrity, and a deep purpose, that is, the kind of leader who brings hope to all of our work. And like a flourishing garden, both the leader and the enterprise can delight and nourish others.

Gardens

The formal landscape stands
ordered monument to mastermind and hands

Each subservient row
disciplined by shear and hoe,

In organic symmetry, sculpted sphere and line,
Not for love of life, but devotion to design

was this infertile illusion crafted
every uniform blade to one will drafted

bearing no largesse to riotous leaf or unruly root,
the master gardener's tyrannous vision absolute.

But, there are other gardens
whose verdant chaos is infested with creative possibility.
Borderless communities of bright souls, they blend, compete,
complement, propagate. Fertile diversity caresses eye and cheek and
olfactory, embracing with equal passion primadonna poppy, dusky
humus, sultry fern, honest grass, each sworn only to
Mendel's oath of self-expression. There is no caretaker here, only
caregivers, inconspicuous in quiet devotion to serve, not control, to
nurture with extravagant love
each unplanned form and unconscious, self-absorbed delight
for the sheer love of life.

Sandy Shugart

CONFRONTING EVIL

DOING GOOD

CONFRONTING EVIL

Better to reign in hell than to serve in heaven.

~ Satan, *Paradise Lost,* John Milton

I ALMOST DIDN'T WRITE THIS ESSAY. AFTER ALL, WHO discusses such a thing as evil in conjunction with our everyday lives and our everyday work? It is far too presumptuous and just a little creepy even to bring up a topic like evil at work, much less to give counsel on how to deal with it. Isn't the word itself a problem? I mean, can't we instead discuss how to deal with mental illness in an employee or colleague? Or at the institutional level, couldn't we address moral and ethical failure in our organizations and leave the language of evil to the Middle Ages where it belongs? Evil is a category that our modern, secular, sanitized, therapeutic, technical minds would rather not have to accommodate. Yet, no one who has lived with his eyes open to the world at large or the ordinary world of work can deny that this is an issue for which we should try to be prepared.

There are people and institutions in our world that have become so twisted, so disoriented, so malevolent that the language of ordinary performance and ethics can't express what they are about nor how we must respond to them. Their existence can't be ignored, and we would do well to have some kind of orientation to dealing with evil when we are confronted with a person or institution that defies any other classification.

I hasten to add that we should be extremely careful before applying such a category to a person or organization. Moralizing the ordinary conflicts and challenges we face at work is almost always a bad idea, alienating others and shutting down the potential for meaningful discourse. The normal categories of such challenges work well in 99.9999 percent of the cases. I have met many people, encountered many organizations that were weak, confused, ill, or misdirected. Most of us have ethical issues to deal with nearly every day in our relationships and in our organizations. These situations require

A conspiracy of silence and a discipline of intentional indifference are required to keep the organization from growing in awareness of the cost of its choices.

a thoughtful ethical orientation, both personal and institutional, a set of principles that are almost automatic and can be consciously brought to bear in discussions of these issues. With the tools of an ongoing ethical discourse, we can generally navigate these situations, though they will often be uncomfortable. This is not what I mean to indicate by the word "evil."

In contrast to these daily experiences of ordinary ethical concerns, I have very, very rarely encountered a person or situation that was different in kind, an entirely different experience. I can count three persons with whom I have worked over the past thirty years who fit this different category, and different they were. Their lives were twisted with delight in causing harm to others. Their minds worked in ways unfathomable to any of their colleagues, and they were treated with amazing delicacy, like a highly venomous snake whose presence could not be altogether avoided but from whom one wanted always to keep a respectful distance. In fact, in all three cases, I and others had a visceral reaction to their presence, hair standing on end, every sense alert to the fact that someone dangerous and unpredictable was in the room.

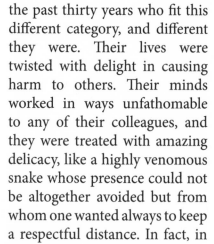

Behind every evil is a backdrop of the pseudo-good, a rationale that makes some sense at the time.

All three of these persons proved self-destructive in the end, but not without taking an almost unbearable toll on others. One undermined the morale of a very fine organization for years, making it her business to exploit any weakness she could find in others to unnerve and dominate them, until she became so untouchable that she was shunned from every place she might have worked. Another secretly exploited the very people he was commissioned to serve until one of them finally had the courage to go public; the perpetrator did not go silently but attempted to wound everyone who got near as he was finally exiled. The third, and most terrible, drew others to him like a spider, knowing from the beginning that he planned eventually to turn and use them if he could. His chosen weapon was the lawsuit. He sued his neighbors, his business partners, his veterinarian, his dentist, his supervisors, his colleagues, even his lawyer. In the end, in the midst of a vicious divorce, he killed himself, but not before murdering his children in order to punish his wife.

Similarly, some organizations and institutions have become so disoriented and self-serving that they choose to ignore the enormous human consequences of their actions and with technical precision and organization visit horrors on others. Perhaps the most studied and monstrous example of this is the Third Reich. Surely if anyone fit the definition of evil, it was Adolph Hitler. But it wasn't just the man that caused forty million horrific deaths and incalculable harm to millions of others. Behind his fiery, hateful rhetoric was a diabolical gift for organization, and it was the organization itself that took on the characteristics of evil, sometimes beyond that of the people running it.

In this kind of twisted organization, ordinary human weaknesses can become servants of the overriding evil of the enterprise. Commenting on this in her powerful analysis *Eichmann in Jerusalem: A Report on the Banality of Evil*, Hannah Arendt wrote, "The deeds were monstrous, but the doer was quite ordinary, commonplace, and neither demonic or monstrous." She wrote that Eichmann was able to send millions to their deaths with no greater motive than his own personal advancement. Similarly, Judge Richard Posner wrote in his scathing analysis of the failure of the German judiciary under the Third Reich that they did evil because they were "so immersed in a professional culture as to be oblivious to the human consequences of their decisions."

These are horrific examples of the larger enterprise driving the actions of hundreds and thousands of others, resulting in unspeakable consequences. Could such institutional evil threaten our places of work? Is it possible for a bureaucracy to become so entangled in its own twisted sense of what is needed to survive and advance that it becomes oblivious to the terrible consequences for other human beings, even the very ones the organization was created to serve? I frankly don't see how a person could work and lead in any part of our criminal justice system, healthcare system, national security system, or any level of government without being aware that the possibility of this kind of institutional evil exists.

My goal in raising these questions is modest. I want first just to put into conversation that we may need a way of discussing evil at work, both at a personal and institutional level, that we may, even in the twenty-first century, need some kind of working theory of evil that enables us to confront these extraordinary circumstances more confidently and effectively. And second, I want to offer just a few practical suggestions on how leaders can prepare for this eventuality, recognizing that when issues of good and evil enter our daily work, the crucible can reach an entirely new level of power, both to form and deform us.

CONFRONTING INSTITUTIONAL EVIL

In our ancient traditions, the task of confronting institutional evil was given to specially gifted leaders called prophets. Their task, in contrast to popular misconception, was not so much foretelling the future, but forth-telling the truth of the present. Thus the Hebrew prophets were generally sent to the leaders of state and religion to declare, at great personal cost, the mindless evil they were engaged in such as oppression of the poor, exploitation of women, injustice to the vulnerable, and idolatry of coveted things over faithfulness to their God and his laws of right living. So the classic definition of prophecy has come to be speaking the truth to power.

> *What is needed in every organization is a willingness to entertain ultimate truth.*

This certainly is a key to confronting the possibility of institutional evil. The peculiar pathology of institutional evil always involves a culture of silence. Upholding the abuses of others requires that they be un-discussable. A conspiracy of silence and a discipline of intentional indifference are required to keep the organization from growing in awareness of the cost of its choices. These can be enforced in many ways: through ignorance of the consequences, refusing to inquire and consider such things; through powerful sanctions or marginalization for anyone brave or foolish enough to raise such a concern; through a language and culture that removes the personal from legitimate organizational concern, reducing approved attention to technical matters only; and through a culture of fear that chills any formal or public consideration of these matters, often belittling the capacity of anyone outside the culture, especially the public, to handle the facts. Confronting institutional evil requires someone to speak up, to legitimize the questions and their discussion at every level of the organization and in public, to make the un-discussable discussable.

We must become deeply convinced of the truth that the organization cannot take us anywhere we clearly refuse to go.

Another key is recognizing that institutional evil always has its own logic, sick though it may be. All manner of evil has been justified by necessity. We all know this logic. It is used to justify covering up terrible truths to protect something deemed to be of more importance—the survival of a company that gives employment to thousands while harming millions; the continuing use of a new drug that may help many, although it has clearly hurt some; the protection of the reputation of the Office of the President. These great institutional lies grow from little lies. Seldom if ever does someone baldly state that an organization should suddenly leap from its normal work into a new malevolent mode of activity. More often, in the normal course of our work, a slow slide into evil is initiated by a series of choices and attendant untruths that may seem necessary in the moment, but put the whole enterprise on a slippery slope requiring one fell step after another toward a future no one would have chosen had they been given the whole decision at once.

This kind of evil thrives on a human condition that seems to deny us the foresight to perceive how one small lie leads to another and another until we find ourselves trapped in a web of lies from which we can only be extricated at great personal cost. It all seems monumentally stupid in retrospect but necessary in the moment of each small choice. Here the crucible is felt keenly in the enormous heat and pressure of trying to survive as the character of our shared work is twisted into something almost unrecognizable and unbearable in the end.

This is another of the common characteristics of evil. The great theological thinker, Gregory of Nyssa, said, "There is no evil other than wickedness." By this he meant that evil is not some independent generative force at work against our natures, but the sum of a series of degenerative bad choices, of wicked decisions, a perversion of the good, a twisting of the familiar.

Though more easily said than done, it is important to remember that the courage to act comes mainly from the heart, not from the head.

Behind every evil is a backdrop of the pseudo-good, a rationale that makes some sense at the time. We resist this analysis because it places all of our work, even our best work, in the crucible where it can ultimately lead, choice by pressured choice, to something terrible that none of us intended. The best medicine for this is to confront the logic of evil at its earliest stages, before the consequences are entirely clear. Our penchant to relativize every choice and treat those who insist on an angular and difficult fidelity to our best principles as awkward moralists, feeds the possibility of the slow slide into genuine wickedness. Hence, the truth of C. S. Lewis's observation through the demon Screwtape's allegorical advice to a junior devil to work gradually with the patient he has been given responsibility for tempting, "the safest path to hell is the gradual one."

What is needed in every organization is a willingness to entertain ultimate truth. I don't mean dogma, but the truly ultimate long-term consequences of flawed moral reasoning even in the case of minor decisions.

"Where will this ultimately lead?" is a question every leader needs to entertain in her daily work.

CONFRONTING PERSONAL EVIL

There is a sense in which all evil is personal. Decisions are made by persons, not organizations. The organization is simply the crucible in which these decisions are made. Therefore, all of the thoughts above about institutional evil have applicability at the personal level. We must become deeply convinced of the truth that the organization cannot take us anywhere we clearly refuse to go. A deep sense of personal responsibility, an unwillingness to just go along with the crowd, is a powerful antidote to institutional evil.

But we may well encounter persons at work who are far beyond any of these personal moral considerations, who have long since surrendered themselves to a way of being that delights in creating trouble, chaos, and suffering, if only they can maintain control. In the final analysis, this may well be a form of mental illness where the only solution for the individual involved, if there is a solution, is deeply therapeutic. But even if this is true, as leaders at work every day, we have to deal fearlessly with such a person on a basis that is not at all therapeutic for them, but designed to protect the innocent from harm and restore health and purpose to the organization.

I say fearlessly because in every case where I have confronted someone this twisted, the situation has been wrapped in fear. Others may fear the ruthlessness of the problem person, her unpredictability and lack of normal boundaries for how she is willing to treat others. Avoidance of the loose cannon is common. Surely it is someone else's responsibility to deal with this person, not mine. We wonder why the organization tolerates the harm she does, forgetting that the organization is just people like us who have taken responsibility and received rewards for its stewardship.

So the first principle in dealing with an evil person is to recognize that it may be a fearsome task and to steel ourselves for this part of the work. Though more easily said than done, it is important to remember that the courage to act comes mainly from the heart, not from the head. I can invent an endless number of reasons to avoid acting, but my heart tells me someone has to stand up and do something for the sake of the many who may be hurt by inaction. I don't mean to make this sound heroic. In fact, heroism has its own pitfalls of pride, self-seeking, attention getting, and personal moral blindness. The action and motivation that are called for include a kind of reluctance, a choice to do something terribly unpleasant and dangerous because it simply needs to be done, in spite of the fear.

What generally needs to be done is simply to banish the evil. This sounds harsh, but a basic characteristic of evil is that we cannot reason with it. In fact, we should avoid even entering into dialogue with evil. Once the problem, that is the person beyond reason, has been identified, it/she must be neutralized, excised like a cancer. This usually means terminating someone's employment and may mean involving other authorities, depending on the person's history. Note that it is especially important for a leader to know that the problem is truly a malignancy here and not the moralizing of a more ordinary personal conflict or performance issue. A leader should take counsel with others who are trustworthy to verify that this is the case.

Second, we should never fight fire with fire. If evil is as evil does, then resorting to the tactics and methods of evil will not only fail to eradicate the problem, it will spread it. Acting with complete integrity when confronting personal evil is essential, giving us the only armor we can take into battle. (Remember how Beowulf was required to descend into the watery home of the monster Grendel's evil mother naked to kill her, weaponless except for his own person?) We can be certain that there will be attempts at retribution, a counterattack whenever we do what has to be done. Therefore, we are enjoined to combine integrity with careful thought about how to make the changes that are necessary. The ancient counsel here, "Be as innocent as doves and as wise as serpents" when dealing with malignancy is worth heeding.

Third, count the cost of the struggle we are engaging when we take on one of these very rare and extreme cases. This means we must be prepared to endure and persist in what may be a protracted struggle. While the deeply twisted person may quickly move on, with no stomach for a decisive altercation and a constant appetite for the path of least resistance, it has been more common in my experience that the hubris of the opponent is boundless, leading to a potentially long and ugly struggle. Again, the objective in these cases is not to reason with the offender, not to improve her performance, and certainly not to make peace with evil, but to remove it and the perpetrator decisively and permanently from a position to do harm. Prepare for action, act decisively, and stubbornly stay the course with all its potential aftermath and fallout. Finally, take special care of your health when dealing with evil – your whole health, mind, body, and spirit. This extreme work takes an extreme toll, and you will need all of your faculties.

The Crucible in Extreme

Dealing with evil, genuinely malevolent forces, whether personal or institutional, creates a crucible experience of the first order, where the potential for deep damage to character—leader's, followers', and organization's—is heightened almost beyond measure. This is dangerous work. It should not be undertaken lightly or, if at all possible, without the thoughtful support of others who have reached a similar conclusion about the character of the conflict we are engaging. Nor should we be too willing to diagnose a problem with a person or organization as one of evil. Even using the word outrages my modern sense of a manageable, predictable, material world where the iron law of cause and effect makes everything ultimately explainable. But there are times, very rare times, when our mechanistic model of the world simply can't account for the data of our experience, and we find that having a working theory of evil is the only way we can make any sense of the most extreme situations we may face as leaders.

As a leader, making highly ethical if difficult decisions, acting only after deep and careful self-examination, and continually inquiring into the effects of this particular kind of conflict on your own heart are essential to your health. Continuing to be mindful in all of these ways will aid in healing the damage caused by the deeply twisted person and the aftereffects of the action to remove her. In dealing with institutional evil, it will also serve to guard your own character as you undergo work that is dangerous not only to your position but to your deep identity.

Remember the heat, pressure, reactivity, and corrosive by-products of the crucible. But also remember the power the crucible has to transform. When someone finally summons the courage to confront and banish wickedness, the lives of many can be powerfully transformed. Our ancient traditions and prayers call this experience "deliverance," as in "deliver us from evil." It is an apt description. I have seen the amazing transformation of whole organizations and many individuals working in them when a long-endured malevolent force was finally removed. They felt delivered. As a friend of mine said after just such an

Acting with complete integrity when confronting personal evil is essential, giving us the only armor we can take into battle.

experience, "I feel like I can breathe again. I had almost forgotten how."

I hope you are never called upon to deal with such a mess, but if you are, be prepared and seek not so much to win in a conflict with an opponent but deliverance and transformation for those suffering with the consequences of a senseless and twisted person or institution so they can get on with the business of doing good.

For these times, knowing how the crucible of work acts upon our characters at work can be a powerful source of wisdom and discretion as we do what has to be done with all the courage we can summon.

Doing Good

Do all the good you can, by all the means you can,
in all the ways you can, in all the places you can,
at all the times you can, to all the people you can,
as long as ever you can.

~ John Wesley

DOING WELL AND DOING GOOD ARE NOT THE same thing. When we go to work, especially when we take on the mantle of leadership—the responsibility to steward an enterprise on behalf of those we serve and those with whom we serve—our co-workers have every reason to expect our best. Our best efforts to lead with and toward excellence come with the role we assume as leader, no matter what the purpose of the organization. This is about doing our jobs well. It is a matter of commitment, competence, and performance. But in addition to doing our work well, it is also of vital importance to our work, ourselves, and our organizations that we do good, seeking both ends and means that are, in a word, a blessing to others.

We needn't look very far to see why this is important to the spirit, both the leader's and the organization's. Stories, our stories, of alienation at work are legendary. Consider the academic department where the scholars in the community are deeply, even viciously divided over amazingly small and arcane matters; or worse, where they have developed a culture of despising the students they are there to serve. Consider the hospital floor where healers may regularly inflict all manner of wounds on one another, and especially those in different and less prestigious roles, through neglect, humiliation, or just ordinary boorishness. Consider the sometimes toxic politics of the local church, where the walking wounded, both ordained and lay people, received their wounds, not in the world, as it were, but in the church itself. In all

In addition to doing our work well, it is also of vital importance to our work, ourselves, and our organizations that we do good, seeking both ends and means that are, in a word, a blessing to others.

of these cases, there is at the core a problem of losing touch with the call to do good even while pursuing the goal of doing well.

Sometimes this issue rises to an almost mythological level. Everyone in our society knows the phrase "going postal." Whether this image has any validity in the facts, that is whether workplace violence is any more likely in the U.S. Postal Service than any other enterprise, is highly doubtful. But the myth has a life of its own, supported, I suspect, not by the actual incidents of workplace violence that have occurred in the USPS, but by our everyday experience of the post office. It isn't even necessary to describe the sense of deadness of spirit and absence of any enthusiasm, much less passion, so apparent in most of the larger urban post offices. It isn't hard to imagine that a few of those once-vital human beings drubbed into lifeless bureaucrats might finally explode in one last violent act of insurrection at work.

Taking seriously the responsibility for at least some of the misery and joy of those with whom we work is essential to the life of every leader.

It hasn't always been this way. The USPS has a deep and honorable history completely inconsistent with the current impression of the deadening bureaucracy. Founded by the Second Continental Congress in 1775, authorized specifically by Article One of the

Constitution and originally led by Benjamin Franklin, the first two hundred years of the USPS were marked by heroic purpose and performance with a reputation that was unimpeachable.

One among many of its more heroic chapters was the creation of the Air Mail Service in 1918. Piloted by intrepid war veterans in surplus de Havilland DH-4 aircraft (get a picture; nothing could be more stirringly romantic), some 1,200 flights were made in the first year, nearly one hundred ending in emergency landings. Yet, within two years, they had delivered more than forty-nine million letters. It is this heroic history that was wrapped up in the public attraction to the famous quotation, "Neither snow nor rain nor heat nor gloom of night stays these couriers from the swift completion of their appointed rounds." (Generally thought of as the USPS motto, it is in fact an inscription on the famous James Farley Post Office in New York City, taken from Herodotus' account of couriers in the ancient Persian Empire. Such is the power of myth.)

The USPS remains an enormous and vital servant institution, though not without serious challenges from the technological revolution and major private sector competition for certain segments of its services. It is one of the largest civilian employer in the country, operating more than a quarter of a million vehicles. It continues, in many ways, to connect the country and bind us into some kind of community across great distances and differences.

So how did we go from the noble myth of the postal service in its first two hundred years of existence to "going postal?" Could the media's sensationalizing of a few tragic incidents of workplace violence and mental illness have created such a popular myth without our common experience of a servant institution that sometimes seems to be in the throes of death by self-strangulation? And would this perception be as strong if we didn't all experience this kind of alienated work wherever we spend the bulk of our workdays?

Alienated Work

Organization kills spirit. (If Robert Greenleaf didn't write this, he should have. I have been unable to find the quote in any of his writings but have an abiding suspicion that this was his idea before it was mine.) Organization kills spirit, and the larger and more complex the organization, the more likely and the more thorough the alienation of those who work in it. Surely, this is a part of what has happened in our story of the USPS. The fact that the tiny, rural post offices often remain lively, responsive centers of community and service suggests as much. But I have a strong suspicion that the size of the monopolistic bureaucracy is only a part of the problem.

I wonder if the depth of alienation isn't also a failure to keep alive what was once a deep sense of doing good, not just doing well, especially in a crucible of work where doing well, where every day's successful performance simply leads to an identical next day, and another, and another. This can describe the repetitive work of a front-line production laborer, a maintenance worker, or a clerk in many industries, but also the life of many a leader, where the expectations can never be fully met and the work can easily become a treadmill.

The workers I know who have remained engaging and joyful in work like this, including "Mudd," our local letter carrier, have a powerful sense of doing good, of making a positive difference in every interaction with co-workers, customers, and others, no matter how incidental to their official job. Mudd befriends the dogs on her route with little illicit snacks, rescues abandoned potted plants from the roadside trash pickup, and bears abroad the best kind of cheerful gossipy concern for the neighbors that reminds us to carry a meal to the lady down the street whom we wouldn't have known was ill, but for Mudd's concern and gabbiness. Mudd finds a way to have fun in her job by looking for ways to be kind and connected to the people around her.

What price do staff members pay when they know there is some good to be done, want to do the good, and don't for no better reason than it might break some rule?

Finding Purpose in Doing Good

This difference in orientation, the commitment to doing good and doing well, has important dimensions at both personal and organizational levels. In both, however, a defining characteristic is a sense of purpose. Purpose is the philosopher's stone that can transform our experience of work and organizational life, even in places where bureaucracy takes on mythological proportions, from a place that is deadening to one that nourishes us with meaning.

We generally fail to consider the good we might accomplish together in the world, not because we couldn't care less, but because the press of daily demands on us squeezes out the habit of reflection.

A strong personal sense of purpose in life is both achievable and perhaps most important when work is the routinized, dumbed-down, standardized labor that has become characteristic of so many jobs since the industrial revolution. The aggregation of effort in mass culture that eliminates our sense of craft by engaging us in procedures and processes rather than ends often puts us in a situation where we work to live, for essentially utilitarian purposes—to put food on the table and pay the bills. There is nothing inherently wrong, or particularly modern, about this kind of work. Nor is it only a pattern in industrial labor.

Many so-called knowledge workers in the post-industrial economy, in fact nearly all service workers, engage in work that requires a minimal exertion of creativity and thought from moment to moment. This doesn't eliminate the crucible effect, the choice between formation and deformation in our day-to-day working lives. Rather, it magnifies it, requiring us to find meaning that isn't altogether apparent in the technical substance or proximate ends of our work. The best and most accessible wisdom in this case is to choose to "do all the good you can to all the people you can" in the midst of what would otherwise be a barren workplace. Also, even in much of the work in which leaders engage, contrary to what we might assume, doing good isn't necessarily an obvious concern until we realize the degree to which we affect the crucibles of other workers in our charge. Keeping this in mind and taking seriously the responsibility for at least some of the misery and joy of those with whom we work is essential to the life of every leader.

I am not suggesting a paternal sense of care for other adults, but sober reflection on the responsibility to humanize the work for others, simply to create a more humane world, and in the process protecting our own sense of humanity and creating a culture more likely to get their best efforts in work that doesn't inherently call forth their commitment by its nature. Sometimes the most important part of our work journey isn't the destination but the fellowship of those with whom we share the road. Doing good enables us to do well over the long term, even if this isn't the highest or only reason to do good.

All I am suggesting is that, bumper-sticker wisdom notwithstanding, our acts of kindness should not be random, but a part of our regular reflection on the nature of our work and how it is forming us and others. To the question, "How well am I doing?" the stuff of performance review, we should always add "What good am I doing?" the stuff of a life that nourishes the soul.

DOING GOOD MEANS ORGANIZATIONAL RISK

I discovered the hard way that there is a special responsibility for leaders here. Quite a few years ago, in my first college presidency, my senior colleagues and I were having just these kinds of discussions and feeling we were beginning to make headway in our organization, a public college of about twenty thousand students. One day a student—we'll call her Jenny—came to see me. She was a "college ambassador" selected for a role representing the college with me in the community, for which she received a modest scholarship and the standard khaki trousers and blue blazer ambassador uniform, and so I was acquainted with this thoughtful student. Jenny was, on this occasion, clearly upset, so I brought her into my office and encouraged her to open up. She told me her boyfriend, with whom I was also acquainted, had been killed two weeks before in an automobile accident. We had a cry, and I offered to do anything I could. She said there was one thing I could do. She had tried coming back to school (this tragedy had occurred mid-semester), but just couldn't complete the term, so she was withdrawing. Further, her finances were very tenuous, so she asked me to arrange a full refund of her tuition. Now, in that particular state, this was actually illegal, the cut-off date for refunds established in the appropriations act by the state legislature. Nevertheless, I promised her a refund and offered to take her textbooks back at full value. Jenny and I talked awhile further, and she left.

During my lunch hour, I was on a long training run with another staff member, several miles from campus, telling him this story. He was not thrilled with it—he was the chief financial officer, a wonderful and caring human being. His concern, I assumed, was the potential of an audit finding, something CFO's hate. I told him not to concern himself, that this was one audit exception I'd be happy to take. (I could just see the headlines: "President Breaks Rules to Help Devastated Student.") "Okay," he said, "but how is this going to make the other staff she talked to feel?" I was stopped dead in my tracks. Of course, I wasn't the first person she had brought this concern to. So we ran back to campus and dressed. I went to see the dean of students. Had she heard from Jenny? Yes, she had. Isn't it awful? She told her there was nothing she could do, but she could come see me if she wanted. Then I went to see the director of admissions, whom I knew to be a friend of Jenny's. Had Jenny come to him? Yes. Isn't it awful? He told her there was nothing he could do, but

Purpose is the philosopher's stone that can transform our experience of work from a place that is deadening to one that nourishes us with meaning.

she could go see the dean if she wanted. So I stopped asking.

I want to emphasize that both the dean and director were and are wonderful people, kind and responsive, always willing to go the extra mile for anyone, and especially for a student in need. Both of them wanted to help her, but it required breaking a rule, creating some risk for the organization and perhaps themselves. They wanted to do good but didn't feel the organization could afford it.

I went back to my office and put my reddened face down on the cool glass desktop, thinking that I had accomplished nothing in two years of leadership. It was my job as the leader to create an environment in my organization where good people could do the right thing for the right reasons fearlessly. And I hadn't. There were two kinds of prices being paid for that failure. People like Jenny who needed our organization to do something good, something special and out of the ordinary, something involving a little bit of risk, were not being served. We were not doing all the good we could to all the people we could. In addition, people like these two staff members were being damaged.

What price do staff members pay when they know there is some good to be done, want to do the good, and don't for no better reason than it might break some rule? We put people in this position all the time. I recall telling this story to a large group of counselors in California who work with students with disabilities every day, coordinating services to support them in their education. Except that the perennial resource limits more often put these people, who entered the work out of a calling to serve, in the position of rationing the services. When I made this point in a rhetorical question, "What price must you be paying in your hearts when this happens?" sobbing could be heard from all over the auditorium.

If we believe in doing all the good we can as a part of our spiritual and psychological health, then we have to create the environment, the organizational culture that permits it, even when it means breaking the rules. We may have to learn how to break the rules intelligently. We may have to clearly give people permission to break the rules. For example, many forward-thinking hospitals have adopted protocols that not only permit, but encourage, nurses to interrupt and challenge a physician they believe may be about to harm a patient through some error or oversight, breaking an unwritten but once inviolable rule. We may even have to pay some consequences for someone else's rule-breaking when it was the right thing to do, like the potential of an audit finding for a broken procedure.

> *We may have to learn to break the rules intelligently.*

This behavior has to be a daily habit, not just a special case.

TRANSCENDENT PURPOSE

If doing good and enabling others to do good is so valuable in our daily jobs, it is all the more important in our thinking about the whole enterprise we are attempting to lead. It is inherent in the experience of the crucible of work that the greater the heat and pressure, the more narrow the focus of our attention becomes. Under pressure to survive and produce, our hierarchy of attention is often forced straight to the bottom line, the tangible and proximate outcomes of our work. We generally fail to consider the good we might accomplish together in the world, not because we couldn't care less, but because the press of daily demands on us squeezes out the habit of reflection, both as individuals and as communities of work. As the poet Rainier Maria Rilke wrote:

> *For somewhere there is an ancient enmity between our daily life and the great work. Help me in saying it to understand it.*
> ~ Rainier Maria Rilke, "Requiem for a Friend"

The source for a deep sense of transcendent purpose in our organizations, the mission beyond the mission, isn't the difference we want to make in the organization or the difference we want to make in the industry, but the difference we want to make in the world. Rarely is this question asked in any serious way in our organizational life. As I sit on various boards of directors, I can imagine the resistance to questions of transcendent purpose as useless distractions and pontificating. But I am certain that these are among the questions that separate great organizations from the mediocre, giving their leadership broader and more meaningful insight into the present and future of the enterprise and calling themselves and their employees to a different sense of pride and commitment to the work.

This isn't just a problem for organizations that are obviously oriented to the bottom line, businesses that are accountable to shareholders looking for added value. In many ways, our servant institutions, with what ought to be clear and transcendent purposes, are even more at risk of avoiding this conversation of ultimate purpose. Saddled by what Robert Greenleaf called "the presumption of virtue," many service-oriented nonprofits regularly fail to carefully consider what good they might do in the world.

Hospitals, pressed by the cost of capital, may pursue operating margins to the exclusion of a deep and regular conversation on ultimate purpose precisely because their underlying purpose is so obviously good. No one could work long in a modern hospital or the criminal justice system or the educational system, however, without realizing how important this conversation can be. Without it, the potential for a great deal of harm (not to mention the "undone good") in pursuit of the obviously good purposes of the institution can go unrecognized and unchecked.

Doing good enables us to do well over the long term.

ASKING THE RIGHT (ULTIMATE) QUESTIONS

Again, it is useful to use language from outside the ordinary discourse of the work world and ask the question, seriously and regularly, "How is our enterprise a blessing to those we serve and those with whom we serve?" We need to know if we are doing all the good we can to all the people we can while we pursue our specific missions with intense focus. The more intensity we bring to our mission, the more crucial the discipline of asking just these questions, or we may awaken someday to an organization that exacts a huge and unnecessary price for its contribution to the world. This is a dimension of corporate ethics that is often overlooked. Deeply ethical corporations don't just attend to whether what they are doing is legal or fair or causing no harm, but whether they are building, or tearing down, the quality of life—substance and spirit—of the world in which they serve.

Many may rail at this entire discussion, but most would also recognize the all too typical organization whose corporate citizenship consists of making contributions out of self-interest, engaging in cause marketing or, even worse, leveraging influential people to do business with them or regulate them differently with actions that masquerade as philanthropy. This isn't citizenship; it is manipulation and politics. Standing in stark contrast are corporations and leaders with a clearly developed sense of the difference they can and want to make in the world and whose citizenship and philanthropy are carefully focused to further this greater good. More importantly, the good they do in these ways isn't some kind of compensation for the harm they are doing in their core mission, but an extension of the good they are seeking to do in all of their work. When asked why they are supporting a cause, the answer flows from their deep mission, not their momentary marketing tactics or the quid pro quo politics of the senior executives, and certainly not to distract the public from their latest disaster.

Deeply ethical corporations don't just attend to whether what they are doing is legal or fair or causing no harm.

There are a number of management experts and economists who object on grounds of theory that this whole discussion is off base. Milton Friedman has argued that even ordinary corporate philanthropy is "subversive," a breach of trust with the shareholders, diminishing the value of their shares and distracting the organization from the only legitimate and final discipline of the market. It is difficult to disagree in theory. But as another of America's great journeyman philosophers said:

> *In theory, there is no difference between theory and practice. But in practice there is.*
> ~ Yogi Berra

What practice suggests is that persons and organizations, in the crucible of work every day, dealing with the pressure, heat, reactivity, and corrosion that is inevitably present in success no less than failure, are subject to deep deformation of their characters. When this goes on unchecked, both can become dysfunctional and even dangerous. Their missions suffer and their performance degrades. In practice, one of the disciplines that can prevent this erosion of spirit and performance is consciously to bring the questions of doing good to bear on our work. In practice, taking seriously the injunction to "do all the good you can to all the people you can" awakens possibilities to connect our purposes and our performance in powerful ways, making it possible both to do well and to do good.

Bonsai II

Great beauties there are in the world
But not all are large.
Some, of course, overwhelm us with length,
Breadth, depth beyond calculation
Bearing in their vastness a story
One can tell only with the
Pure forms of mathematics
Tracing wave and particle
Into the impossibly remote past.
Some only an angstrom's length,
Embellish a work beneath the surface of sight
Their careful, improbable symmetry
Visible only to those few
So trained to unmovable observation
They can no longer see what
Is clearly written in
The delicate design.
But here is one we can easily apprehend and love,
Possessing in its kindly scale
All the organic warmth and wisdom
We would embrace
Suggesting many years lived
Recalling a weightiness rooted in
Solid earth and reaching
Beyond itself.
Like a simple, unexpected, unjustifiable
Act of kindness, lost in the order of magnitudes
Of the great universal signs,
But all the more clearly enlightening
The space where we actually live.

Sandy Shugart

POSTLUDE

DOING OUR
FIRST WORK

WE'VE COME A LONG WAY TOGETHER. MANY years have passed since my first real epiphany on the power of work to shape or misshape us, as I described it in the prologue. If you have gotten this far, there are a couple of rather remarkable surprises I need to acknowledge. The first is that this book got published at all. I don't say this out of the usual doubts and challenges that attend any creative act, including writing even a short book, though there have been a few. What is surprising is that a book that doesn't claim to have all the answers could find its way through a world of publishing that sells answers.

More than once, someone has tried to make of this a how-to book—the five principles of authenticity or the three steps to being really effective at work or whatever.

Apparently this is what the market demands, what sells and gets handed out by all the frustrated senior managers to all the frustrated middle managers, and so on down the line. People under pressure and frustrated by the complexities and intransigence of their working lives want answers, simple answers, direct answers. We want a procedure to follow that will guarantee results. We want a new and improved technique for improving our work and our lives. Who wouldn't?

In fact, if the daily experience of working and leading were just about getting the right procedure and technique, no one would need a book like this, a book that calls us to a deeper conversation with ourselves, our work, and our world. If the last hundred or so years of scientific management and its progeny have taught us anything, though, it is that working and leading effectively and meaningfully requires much, much more than good procedures, much more than technique.

To be genuinely healthy in our work and in our leading requires a kind of mindfuless.

To be genuinely healthy in our work and in our leading requires a kind of mindfulness, an integration or weaving back together of the various strands of our selves, even as the crucible of work tries to fractionate and strip them apart. Rather than living out roles that have been given to us, and those segregated into relatively separate compartments, the philosopher's stone for our working lives is a call to wholeness, to a way of working and being that acknowledges how connected the parts of our lives are and ought to be. This requires of us something that is at once simple and difficult: that we hold ourselves, our work, and our organizations up to constant and probing reflection. Or perhaps it is more apt to say we engage ourselves in fiercely honest and ongoing conversation, interior and exterior conversations, out of which wisdom may emerge, if we endure in this our first and most important work. There are no standard steps, no procedures for this. It is, though, a way of being that can be cultivated, and every unique human being has the capacity for this self-regarding discipline. Few, however, practice it. So, I am surprised this book has been published.

We must engage ourselves in fiercely honest and ongoing conversations, interior and exterior, out of which wisdom may emerge.

A second surprise is that I have been the one to write it. Anyone who knows me will readily recognize how much work I have yet to do in all of the areas I have brought to you in these essays, and in many other areas of my imperfect life. More than once I have been tempted to put the manuscript down and wait for someone more qualified in wisdom, experience, and success in living out this kind of mindful life in the crucible to write about it. So these essays are offered to you and your further reflection as a few notes from the road, a journey I hope we now share and along which you may already have progressed much further than I.

Finally, I have been deeply and pleasantly surprised by the warmth and intensity of response to these thoughts as they have been shared in lectures and homilies, essays, and luncheon conversations over the past several years. Apparently, this is a conversation for which many have hungered, and if you have joined it, you now bear a responsibility to carry it to your own private interior workshop and to others who may be hungering for it as well. I am certain that I have only scratched the surface of the topic. I hope, though, that I have managed to raise a few of those questions David Whyte mentioned in his poem "Sometimes:"

> "...questions that can make or unmake a life,
> ...questions that have waited patiently for you,
> ...questions that have no right to go away."

ACKNOWLEDGEMENTS

No book is ever the product of just one person's effort, least of all a first book. In this case, I have more people to thank because the book is the product of many years of experience "in the crucible" with others, from whom I have learned most of what I know of leadership. Some were conscious examples; others never knew how much I was learning from their work and our long conversations.

To those who know you were mentors to me, and those who didn't, I offer my profound thanks: to Curtis Shugart, Carl Shugart, and John Zabel, who had the earliest and most lasting impact; to Bobby Gross, Steve Quakenbush, Ellison Jones, and Jim Long, who planted the seeds of servant leadership in what must have looked like very poor soil; to Bob Scott, George Fouts, Kathy Baker Smith, Jim Hunt, Roger Worthington, Ed Wilson, and Tom King, who taught me to think like a leader and endured my youth with good humor; to John Pickelman, Steve Head, Bill Law, Olin Joynton, Clark Lowenfield, and Patsy Gray, who stuck with me when the crucible was at its worst; and to Mark Milliron, Gerardo de los Santos, Jackson Sasser, Byron McClenney and Kaye McCelenney, who have been fellow travellers and friends in this work.

A number of people have been exceptionally generous with their time, reading drafts and counseling me on this project. I especially wish to thank Brian Paradis, Ellison Jones, Sherri Sitarik, Jackson Sasser, and again, Byron McClenney, Kay McClenney, and Curtis Shugart for their insights and patience.

Throughout the editing process I have been blessed with great professional guidance – special thanks to Todd Chobotar, Cynthia Wilson, and the critical readers who helped to refine the work and offered encouragement that this manuscript might be more than something I needed to write, actually benefitting a few who might read it. In addition, thanks are due to both the League for Innovation and Florida Hospital for their official and personal connection to the work.

Finally, for their patience and support, I thank my family, especially my wife of more than 33 years, Jane, who never wondered whether I would finish what I had started, even when I did.

Sandy Shugart
Soli Deo Gloria

ABOUT THE AUTHOR

SANFORD C. "SANDY" SHUGART, PHD, STUMBLED INTO SENIOR leadership at a very early age and found himself "in the deep end, with sharks." As vice president of a billion dollar higher education system and twenty years the junior of any of his colleagues and staff, he was compelled to learn to lead in a hurry. What he discovered was a powerful interaction between the challenges of his work as a leader and the formation of his character.

Dr. Shugart's leadership journey took him on to presidencies of two large colleges, an active life of speaking on these issues in the US and Europe, a visiting scholars chair at Oxford University, and various boards of directors. In all of these roles, he has been in the laboratory of leadership, in the crucible of pressure, heat, and reactivity that defines modern organizational life and acts powerfully to form or to deform the deep character of the leader and the led.

His reflections on these experiences have informed his own leadership roles, his poetry, and his music for many years. Most of all, he is a storyteller, sharing with good humor and humility the inner struggles he and many other leaders confront every day.

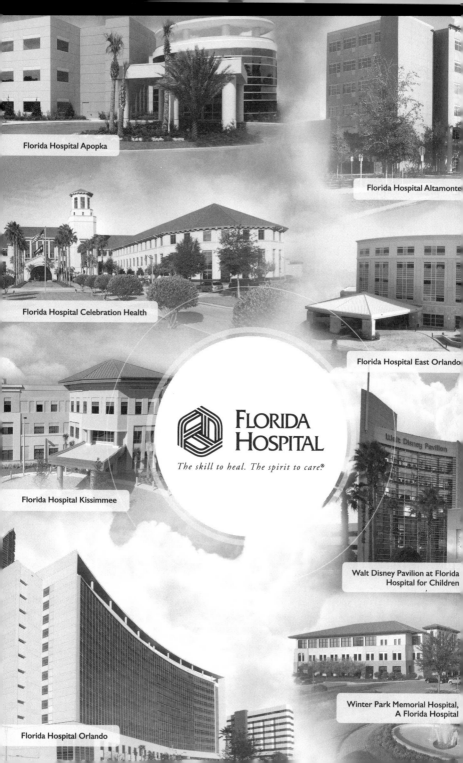

Florida Hospital Apopka

Florida Hospital Altamonte

Florida Hospital Celebration Health

Florida Hospital East Orlando

FLORIDA HOSPITAL

The skill to heal. The spirit to care.®

Florida Hospital Kissimmee

Walt Disney Pavilion at Florida Hospital for Children

Winter Park Memorial Hospital, A Florida Hospital

Florida Hospital Orlando

ABOUT THE PUBLISHER

For over one hundred years the mission of Florida Hospital has been: To extend the healing ministry of Christ. Opened in 1908, Florida Hospital is comprised of eight hospital campuses housing over 2,400 beds and twenty-two walk-in medical centers. With over 19,000 employees—including 2,200 doctors and 6,600 nurses—Florida Hospital serves the residents and guests of Orlando, the No. 1 tourist destination in the world. Florida Hospital has over 1.7 million patient visits a year. Florida Hospital is a Christian, faith-based hospital that believes in providing Whole Person Care to all patients – mind, body, and spirit. Hospital fast facts include:

LARGEST ADMITTING HOSPITAL IN AMERICA.
Ranked No. 1 in the nation for inpatient admissions by the American Hospital Association.

AMERICA'S HEART HOSPITAL.
Ranked No. 1 in the nation for number of heart procedures performed each year, averaging 22,000 cases annually. MSNBC named Florida Hospital "America's Heart Hospital" for being the No. 1 hospital fighting America's No. 1 killer—heart disease.

HOSPITAL OF THE FUTURE.
At the turn of the century, the Wall Street Journal named Florida Hospital the "Hospital of the Future".

ONE OF AMERICA'S BEST HOSPITALS.
Recognized by U.S. News & World Report as "One of America's Best Hospitals" for ten years. Clinical specialties recognized have included: Cardiology, Orthopaedics, Neurology & Neurosurgery, Urology, Gynecology, Digestive Disorders, Hormonal Disorders, Kidney Disease, Ear, Nose & Throat and Endocrinology.

LEADER IN SENIOR CARE.
Florida Hospital serves the largest number of seniors in America through Medicare with a goal for each patient to experience a "Century of Health" by living to a healthy hundred.

TOP BIRTHING CENTER.
Fit Pregnancy magazine named Florida Hospital one of the "Top 10 Best Places in the Country to have a Baby". As a result, The Discovery Health Channel struck a three-year production deal with Florida Hospital to host a live broadcast called "Birth Day Live." Florida Hospital annually delivers over 10,000 babies.

CORPORATE ALLIANCES.
Florida Hospital maintains corporate alliance relationships with a select group of Fortune 500 companies including Disney, Nike, Johnson & Johnson, Philips, AGFA, and Stryker.

DISNEY PARTNERSHIP.
Florida Hospital is the Central Florida health & wellness resource of the Walt Disney World® Resort. Florida Hospital also partnered with Disney to build the ground breaking health and wellness facility called Florida Hospital Celebration Health located in Disney's town of Celebration, Florida. Disney and Florida Hospital recently partnered to build a new state-of-the-art Children's Hospital.

HOSPITAL OF THE 21ST CENTURY.
Florida Hospital Celebration Health was awarded the Premier Patient Services Innovator Award as "The Model for Healthcare Delivery in the 21st Century".

SPORTS EXPERTS.
Florida Hospital is the official hospital of the Orlando Magic NBA basketball team. In addition, Florida Hospital has an enduring track record of providing exclusive medical care to many sports organizations. These organizations have included: Disney's Wide World of Sports, Walt Disney World's Marathon Weekend, the Capital One Bowl, and University of Central Florida Athletics. Florida Hospital has also provided comprehensive healthcare services for the World Cup and Olympics.

CONSUMER CHOICE AWARD WINNER.
Florida Hospital has received the Consumer Choice Award from the National Research Corporation every year from 1996 to the present.

PUBLICATIONS.
Florida Hospital Publishing can help you live life to the fullest with a variety of health and wellness books and other resources uniquely focused on Whole Person Health. Visit: www.FloridaHospitalPublishing.com

601 E. Rollins Street, Orlando, FL 32803
FloridaHospital.org | 407-303-5600

LEAD YOUR COMMUNITY
TO HEALTHY
LIVING

INCLUDES ONLINE TRAINING

Seminar Leader Kit
Everything a leader needs to conduct this seminar successfully, including key questions to facilitate group discussion and PowerPoint™ presentations for each of the eight principles.

Participant Guide
A study guide with essential information from each of the eight lessons along with outlines, self-assessments, and questions for people to fill in as they follow along.

Small Group Kit
It's easy to lead a small group using the CREATION Health videos, the Small Group Leader Guide, and the Small Group Discussion Guide.

CREATION Kids
CREATION Health Kids can make a big difference in homes, schools, and congregations. Lead kids in your community to healthier, happier living.

Life Guide Series
These guides include questions designed to help individuals or small groups study the depths of every principle and learn strategies for integrating them into everyday life.

The Love Fight (Softcover)

Are you going to fight for love or against each other? In *The Love Fight*, Drs. Tony Ferretti and Peter Weiss address a new dichotomy: the clash between Achievers and Connectors. The authors illustrate how this common encounter can create a mutually satisfying relationship. Their expertise will walk you through the scrimmage between those who want to accomplish and those who want to relate.

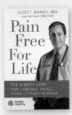

Pain Free For Life (Hardcover)

In *Pain Free For Life*, Scott C. Brady, MD,—founder of Florida Hospital's Brady Institute for Health—shares his dramatically successful solution for chronic back pain, fibromyalgia, chronic headaches, irritable bowel syndrome, and other "impossible to cure" pains. Dr. Brady leads pain-racked readers to a pain-free life using powerful mind-body-spirit strategies—where more than 80 percent of his chronic-pain patients have achieved 80–100 percent pain relief within weeks.

If Today Is All I Have (Softcover)

At its heart, Linda's captivating account chronicles the struggle to reconcile her three dreams of experiencing life as a "normal woman" with the tough realities of her medical condition. Her journey is punctuated with insights that are at times humorous, painful, provocative, and life-affirming.

SuperSized Kids (Hardcover)

In *SuperSized Kids*, Walt Larimore, MD, and Sherri Flynt, MPH, RD, LD, show how the mushrooming childhood obesity epidemic is destroying children's lives, draining family resources, and pushing America dangerously close to a total healthcare collapse—while also explaining, step by step, how parents can work to avert the coming crisis by taking control of the weight challenges facing every member of their family.

SuperFit Family Challenge – Leader's Guide

Perfect for your community, church, small group, or other settings.
The SuperFit Family Challenge Leader's Guide Includes:

- Eight weeks of pre-designed PowerPoint™ presentations.
- Professionally designed marketing materials and group handouts from direct mailers to reading guides.
- Training directly from Author Sherri Flynt, MPH, RD, LD, across six audio CDs.
- Media coverage and FAQ on DVD.

Forgive To Live (English: Hardcover / Spanish: Softcover)

In *Forgive to Live* Dr. Tibbits presents the scientifically proven steps for forgiveness—taken from the first clinical study of its kind conducted by Stanford University and Florida Hospital.

Forgive To Live Workbook (Softcover)

This interactive guide will show you how to forgive – insight by insight, step by step—in a workable plan that can effectively reduce your anger, improve your health, and put you in charge of your life again, no matter how deep your hurts.

Forgive To Live Devotional (Hardcover)

In his powerful new devotional, Dr. Dick Tibbits reveals the secret to forgiveness. This compassionate devotional is a stirring look at the true meaning of forgiveness. Each of the fifty-six spiritual insights includes motivational Scripture, an inspirational prayer, and two thought-provoking questions. The insights are designed to encourage your journey as you begin to *Forgive to Live*.

Forgive To Live God's Way, A Small Group Resource (Softcover)

Forgiveness is so important that our very lives depend on it. Churches teach us that we should forgive, but how do you actually learn to forgive? In this spiritual workbook, noted author, psychologist, and ordained minister Dr. Dick Tibbits takes you step-by-step through an eight-week forgiveness format that is easy to understand and follow.

Forgive To Live Leader's Guide

Perfect for your community, church, small group, or other settings.
The Forgive To Live Leader's Guide Includes:

- Eight weeks of pre-designed PowerPoint™ presentations.
- Professionally designed customizable marketing materials and group handouts on CD-Rom.
- Training directly from author of *Forgive to Live* Dr. Dick Tibbits across six audio CDs.
- Media coverage DVD.
- CD-Rom containing all files in digital format for easy home or professional printing.
- A copy of the first study of its kind conducted by Stanford University and Florida Hospital showing a link between decreased blood pressure and forgiveness.

CREATION Health Discovery (Softcover)

CREATION Health Discovery takes the 8 essential principles of CREATION Health and melds them together to form the blueprint for the health we yearn for and the life we are intended to live.

CREATION Health Breakthrough (Hardcover)

Blending science and lifestyle recommendations, Monica Reed, MD, prescribes eight essentials that will help reverse harmful health habits and prevent disease. Discover how intentional choices, rest, environment, activity, trust, relationships, outlook, and nutrition can put a person on the road to wellness. Features a three-day total body rejuvenation therapy and four-phase life transformation plan.

CREATION Health Devotional for Women (English)

Written for women by women, the *CREATION Health Devotional for Women* is based on the principles of whole-person wellness represented in CREATION Health. Spirits will be lifted and lives rejuvenated by the message of each unique chapter. This book is ideal for women's prayer groups, to give as a gift, or just to buy for your own edification and encouragement.

A Desk Reference to Personalizing Patient Care (Hardcover)

Aurora Realin, MBA, CDM, discusses how diversity is increasing at a rapid pace. Clinicians committed to providing the best patient care must become familiar with the key attitudes and expectations of patients whose culture, religious beliefs, generation, or level of disability differs from their own.

Now there is help. *Personalizing Patient Care* is a valuable guide for improving a caregiver's understanding of how a patient's background may affect their needs, preferences, and expectations related to the delivery of care.

HEAR MORE FROM Dr. Sandy Shugart

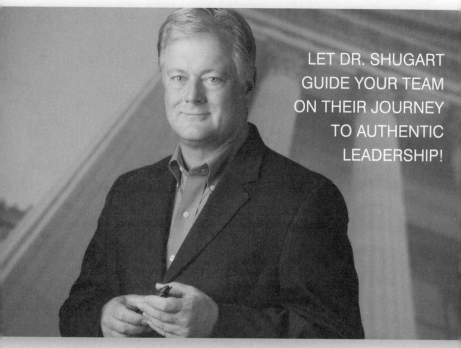

LET DR. SHUGART
GUIDE YOUR TEAM
ON THEIR JOURNEY
TO AUTHENTIC
LEADERSHIP!

Dr. Shugart Speaks on Many Topics Including:

- **Changing the Conversation**
  Leading Deep Cultural Change in your Organization

- **Authentic Service**
  Recovering the Power of Persons in your Service Culture

- **Work as Spiritual Formation**
  A Working Theology of Work

- **Listening Well As A Leader**
  The keys to communication that lead to deeper connections

- **A Leader's Failure Analysis**
  Discover the 5 questions that will help you learn from failure

- **Being Detached, Staying Engaged**
  The art of not losing yourself in leadership

- **Navigating the Storms**
  4 principles that will help your organization navigate even the heaviest of seas

To book Dr. Shugart or another speaker for your event, visit
www.FloridaHospitalPublishing.com